Berlitz

BRUSSELS

POCKET GUIDE

C000144335

Walking Eye
mobile app

Discover the world's best destinations with the Insight Guides Walking Eye app, available to download for free in the App Store and Google Play.

The container app provides easy access to fantastic free content on events and activities taking place in your current location or chosen destination, with the possibility of booking, as well as the regularly-updated Insight Guides travel blog: Inspire Me. In addition, you can purchase curated, premium destination guides through the app, which feature local highlights, hotel, bar, restaurant and shopping listings, an A to Z of practical information and more. Or purchase and download Insight Guides eBooks straight to your device.

TOP 10 ATTRACTIONS

THE CATHÉDRALE DES STS-MICHEL-ET-GUDULE
Beautiful stained glass windows in the choir depict Louis II and his wife. See page 38.

MANNEKEN-PIS
The city's famously cheeky statue. See page 37.

ATOMIUM
A symbol of the city, this metallic 1950s sculpture rises above the toy-town buildings of Mini-Europe. See page 56.

THE OLD ENGLAND DEPARTMENT STORE
One of many lovely Art Nouveau buildings, it now houses a music museum. See page 43.

THE GRAND-PLACE
This focal point of the city's daily life is simply one of the loveliest squares in the world. See page 30.

GHENT
The city has numerous attractions, including the picturesque Korenlei. See page 83.

PLACE ROYALE
The square at the heart of Royal Brussels. See page 41.

PARC DU CINQUANTENAIRE
Beautiful formal gardens with a monumental arch created for King Leopold II. See page 51.

ANTWERP'S GROTE MARKT
The central fountain depicts Antwerp's hero Silvius Brabo. See page 64.

BRUGES
The 13th-century Belfry towers over the old town. See page 72.

A PERFECT DAY

9.00am

Breakfast
Begin the day in style
by having breakfast
at the terrace café of
the sumptuous Belle
Époque-style Métropole
Hotel, on place de
Brouckère.

11.00am

A stroll through central Brussels
Walk to the Galeries Royales St-Hubert, an elegant
19th-century shopping arcade, emerging below the
Gothic Cathédral des Sts-Michel-et-Gudule. Then go
past Gare Centrale to the Mont des Arts, a fine city
garden and restored showcase of 1950s architecture.
Drop downhill through place St-Jean to view
Manneken-Pis, and decide for yourself whether this
much-loved symbol of Brussels is worth all the fuss.
Return to the Grand-Place.

1.00pm

Lunch
There are many
restaurants in the l'Ilot
Sacré district just off the
Grand-Place, but you
can't do better than join
the throng for lunch in
the traditional Belgian
restaurant 'T Kelderke,
set in an atmospheric
Grand-Place cellar.

10.00am

The Grand-Place
Walk to the Grand-Place by way of place de la
Monnaie, passing the Théâtre Royal de la Monnaie,
the city's neoclassical opera and ballet house, on
the way. When you arrive at the Grand-Place, take
in the magnificent spectacle as an ensemble. Then,
going around the square, take time to view the ornate
facades of the buildings, including the Hotel de Ville,
Maison du Roi and guildhouses.

IN **BRUSSELS**

4.00pm

Two squares
Along rue de la Régence are place du Grand-Sablon and place du Petit-Sablon, the former home to fine antiques stores and a weekend antiques market, the latter a neat little park.

5.00pm

Avenue Louise
By tram or on foot you pass by the city's vast Palais de Justice, looming above the atmospheric but poor Marolles quarter. Place Louise marks the start of avenue Louise, a long boulevard rich in upmarket shops. Along the way, rest your legs over a drink in a hotel, such as the Steigenberger Wiltcher's hotel.

7.00pm

Indian dinner
Since you had a Belgian-style lunch, consider taking a tram or taxi to the far end of avenue Louise, for dinner at the superb Indian restaurant La Porte des Indes.

9.00pm

A Brussels café
If you're up for a pre-sleep drink, head back to the city centre, to that grande dame of Brussels bars, À la Mort Subite, a few streets from the Grand-Place, and order a traditional Brussels beer, such as a *gueuze*.

2.00pm

A choice of museums
Take a stroll through the Parc de Bruxelles. Emerging on its south side at place Royale, visit Belgium's premier art museum, the Musées Royaux des Beaux-Arts, or focus instead on the nearby Musée Magritte, dedicated to the work of Belgium's great surrealist painter.

CONTENTS

INTRODUCTION

Brussels is the capital of Belgium, a small country of 11.5 million people set between the Netherlands in the north, France in the south and Germany in the east. The city lies roughly in the centre of the country, and along the line that divides Belgium into Dutch-speaking Flanders in the north and French-speaking Wallonia in the south. When Belgium gained its independence in 1830, Brussels was at first cast in a purely domestic role. Since the end of World War II, however, this city of close to two million has evolved into an international centre. The headquarters of NATO are here, and the city is the focal point of the European Union (EU). Brussels is a truly international city, where most people speak at least two languages, demand for office space is sky-high and the international airport is one of the fastest-growing in Europe.

HISTORIC TOWN

Small by international standards – the city centre can be crossed on foot in about 30 minutes – Brussels is decidedly people-friendly. It has a buoyant native population that fills the streets with vibrancy by day and makes it one of the world's safest major cities by night. It is a city of delights, and one that surprises with its architecture, gastronomy and nightlife.

Brussels has been at the heart of European history for much of the last millennium. A trading town on the lucrative route from Eastern Europe to England, it was the leading northern city of the vast Spanish European Empire during the 17th century and, after Vienna, of the wealthy Habsburg Austro-Hungarian Empire in the 18th century. However, though Brussels continues to flirt with Europe, it is first and foremost a Belgian city.

TRADING PLACES

In addition to being a diplomatic centre, it has always
been a working and trad-
ing town. The pearl that is
the old heart of Brussels
began its life around the
seed of a marketplace in
the 14th century. You will
discover that many of the
street names in the old town
hark back to this time, when
traders would set up stalls
along the narrow, cobbled
alleys. Cheese Market,
Chicken Market, Grass

The Town Hall on the Grand-Place

Market and Butchers' Row – the names conjure up images of bustling medieval Brussels. These same streets still earn their keep,
sustaining modern visitors with bars and restaurants. The guilds
that controlled the skilled trades built large and ornate houses
in the centre of town as a visual affirmation of their wealth and
influence. They extended a largely benevolent but, when required,
brutal control over Brussels' artisans, who were admired around
Europe for their skill and workmanship. On Coudenberg, a hill
east of the old town, sat royal and ducal palaces and buildings to
house visiting foreign emissaries sent to negotiate with the occu-
pants of the neighbouring palaces.

A 17th-century town square, the Grand-Place, takes one's
breath away with its ornate stonework and gilt decoration. The
14th-century Town Hall is one of the most beautiful examples of
civic architecture in Europe. And the narrow streets that surround
it are replete with original architectural detail. The skyline on the

European institutions

hill above was transformed during the 18th century in the Louis XVI style. The palace is still in use by today's Belgian royal family, but it now sits side-by-side with museums dedicated to the arts, filled with collections encompassing the finest Belgian artists and canvasses by European masters. In the 19th century, King Leopold II gave life to a number of civil construction projects; and in the 20th century, Brussels continued to make architectural history with the futuristic Atomium (completed in 1958, just in time for Brussels to host the World's Fair). Almost every corner of the city offers an architectural treat: from Romanesque churches to Gothic towers and Baroque theatres, and a wealth of Art Nouveau – in fact no architecture buff should leave Brussels dissatisfied.

NATIVES AND FOREIGNERS
Thanks to the presence of the EU and NATO, it is said that there are more decision-makers here than in any other city on earth.

And yet, when you walk the streets, Brussels does not feel like a powerhouse. It has the gentility and civility of a dowager duchess and it never seems to throw its considerable weight around. Perhaps this is because, even today, the city is not only concerned about world affairs. For every foreign diplomat, there is a shopkeeper, and this 'real activity' helps the city to maintain its pragmatic air.

There is relatively little friction between the natives and the 'army' of foreigners who make Brussels their temporary home. But then this isn't the first foreign 'invasion' to confront the city. The character of the city and its people has been shaped by their country's geography, sandwiched as it has been between two seemingly constantly warring dynasties. Numerous decisive battles have taken place on Belgian soil, Waterloo being but one. Foreigners have usurped this land on many occasions, including both world wars. Today's bloodless diplomatic 'coups' are designed to consign all of this to history.

In the midst of European détente, Belgium's internal strife may astonish visitors, but with several disparate groups making up the population, differences of opinion on language, education and social services are still being fought out in council chambers and the press. The Flemish north of the country is Dutch-speaking and the Walloon south is French-speaking; the tension between the two communities has threatened the country's very existence. There is also a small German-speaking enclave in the east.

Despite this domestic friction, the Belgians have a

Underground art

The Brussels metro provides transport – and more. Art has gone underground, transforming commuter platforms with a wealth of colour and style. All the works on display are by famous Belgian artists.

philosophical attitude to life. There's a great deal to like about people who decorate their metro stations with canvasses by their best known contemporary artists, and the sides of houses with cartoon or comic-strip images. Their love of imagery makes Brussels rich in cinema, photography, sculpture and art. With national ballet, opera and theatre companies, there is no shortage of high art, but in addition Brussels embraces with ease novel genres and groundbreaking work.

When Belgians do things, they do them with a passion. Where else would you be able to choose from around 800 different domestic beers, or eat mussels cooked in 20 different styles? The many restaurants and bars in the city pay testament to Brussels' love of the good life.

This passion has also extended to collecting, with a multitude of museums to explore. Although many attractions are found in the city centre, many others are located within the 19 *communes* or districts that make up the Brussels-Capital Region. These are only a short tram ride away, or one or two stops on the metro. Each commune has a particular character – from tree-lined bourgeois districts to gritty working-class neighbourhoods. As Europe has extended a helping hand to refugees from many countries, some areas now have burgeoning African, Asian and Arab populations. Exploring at least one of these *communes* allows you to discover more of the real Brussels; for underneath its charms – the majestic old buildings, impressive museum collections and pretty streets – the city has a complex and alluring personality.

Brussels is full of surprises. City dwellers have vast swathes of forest to enjoy, just a tram ride from the city centre. To those who expect bland Euroland, Brussels presents a historical time capsule. And to those who imagine a living museum, they discover a 21st-century society thoroughly in tune with the 'now'. So soak it up – it's rare to find a place where this combination works so well.

A BRIEF HISTORY

In 57BC, Julius Caesar came to Belgium and, after a great deal of trouble with a population he described as 'the bravest of all the peoples of Gaul', conquered the country. At that time, Brussels did not yet exist as a city, although two Roman roads had been built through its present site (one of which is still called chaussée Romaine). From the evidence of the bronzes, coins and funeral urns found, a number of dignitaries and officers had villas constructed in the area some decades later. During the 450 years of Roman rule, the Belgae of the southern region became heavily Latinised, while the north was left in the end to Germanic tribes.

Brussels first appeared on the scene around AD600 when St Géry, the Bishop of Cambrai, is said to have built a church at the small settlement here. At this time and later, it was known variously as Brosella, Brucella, Bruocsella, Bruohsella, Bruesella and Borsella, with as many different meanings suggested by historians. Selections include 'stork's nest' and 'dwelling near the bridge', but the most generally accepted seems to be 'dwelling in the marshes'.

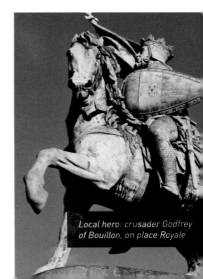

Local hero: crusader Godfrey of Bouillon, on place Royale

This supposedly refers to three swampy islands in the now paved-over River Senne, on which the first castle and church were built.

THE MIDDLE AGES

The foundation of the city proper dates back officially to AD979, when a fortress was erected here by Charles, Duke of Lower Lorraine, the brother of Carolingian King Lothair of France. In the following century, the town began to take shape when, in 1047, Count Lambert II of Leuven (Louvain) built a new castle on the Coudenberg Heights (today called place Royale), surrounded by a group of houses within a walled compound. The lack of space inside meant that artisans and peasants were left unprotected outside the ramparts, thus laying the foundations for the long struggle between the city's haves and have-nots.

⊙ THE RIVER SENNE

Most major cities have a body of water nearby. They may be seaports, or set on river mouths, or at crossing points on rivers inland. But Brussels does not have a river. Or does it?

Well, in fact, it does. The city was originally founded on the River Senne, whose path cut directly through the centre of the old town. However, when the river became dirty and polluted following the Industrial Revolution, the people of Brussels decided on a novel and innovative solution; they would simply put the river out of sight. Work began in 1867 and was allied with a comprehensive plan by Mayor Jules Anspach to create a number of fine boulevards in the newly created landscape above. A series of culverts confined the waters and a network of sewers drained effluent from all parts of the city. Finally, the river disappeared under brick arcades, although it still flows to the present day.

In the 12th century, Brussels rose to prominence in the province of Brabant, gaining in prosperity due to its role as a centre of gold and silver-smithing and as a station on the commercial route between the trading centres of Cologne and Bruges. By 1235 the city's administration was in the hands of an oligarchy of seven patrician families known as *lignages*. Each contributed an *échevin*, or alderman,

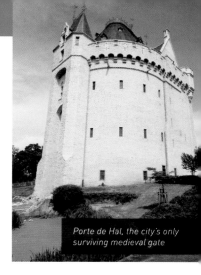

Porte de Hal, the city's only surviving medieval gate

to serve on the council. Brussels expanded its trade in precious metals with international orders for minting coins. It also started a prosperous textile industry using wool imported from England. However, with male workers demanding higher wages and better working conditions, the lords began to look elsewhere for labour, and a number of *béguinages* (communities of religious lay women) were established, partly as a source of cheap and docile workers.

The Brussels bourgeoisie was already growing prosperous and willful. In 1291 Duke Jean I had to make tax and toll concessions to their municipal treasury. In an attempt to forestall the problems of dealing with recalcitrant artisans, the ruling oligarchy claimed the right of approval over the formation of the craft guilds–a restriction that strongly riled the artisans.

The Brussels craftsmen staged a revolt demanding a greater say in city government. Some 36 professional groups were each allowed to send representatives to administer the town's affairs.

However, Brussels' first attempt at democracy came to an abrupt end just three years later, when the army of Duke Jean II and the patrician cavalry of the *lignages* defeated the artisans in the bloody battle of Vilvoorde (1306). For the next 50 years the artisans were forbidden to bear arms, and uprisings rumbled on until guild privileges were gradually reinstated for certain professions.

THE BURGUNDIANS

At the end of the 14th century the dukes of Burgundy took control of Brussels from their seat in Bruges, and under them good times were to be had. However, the demand for Brussels cloth declined, as at the same time textiles manufactured in England became more competitive. By 1430 Brussels cloth had practically disappeared from international markets. With no work, many artisans were forced to leave the city, and the population declined. Brussels compensated for the collapse of the textile industry by turning to tapestry weaving, for which it became renowned. The demand for skilled Brussels weavers became intense. With demand rising for other skills as well, the craft guilds began to reform and gain strength.

The Burgundian era was a golden age for the arts. Jan van Eyck, Rogier van der Weyden, Hans Memling and Dirk Bouts were only

Charles the Bold

the best known of a superb group of 15th-century Flemish paint-ers. Civic pride was reflected in the great Gothic town halls that sprang up all across Belgium, though none ever surpassed Brussels' own great jewel in the Grand-Place, surrounded by equally grand guild houses.

The dukes – Philip the Bold, John the Fearless, Philip the Good and Charles the Bold –asserted their supremacy with pageants and festivities to keep the people happy. However, their dominance began to disintegrate in wars with Louis XI of France, and before long the city was beset with revolts, famine and plague. Charles the Bold, Philip the Good's successor, was in turn succeeded by his daughter Mary, who married Maximilian of Austria and thus brought the Habsburgs to Brussels.

HABSBURG RULE

In 1515 Maximilian's grandson, the future Charles V, made his *Joyeuse Entrée* into Brussels as its new archduke. He moved into the palace on the Coudenberg, which was to be his only fixed residence during his peripatetic reign as king of Spain and Holy Roman Emperor. As Bruges lost its influence, Brussels became the capital of the Low Countries (roughly fol-lowing the borders of what is now Belgium and Holland), as well as a great European centre of trade and culture.

The renowned Dutch philosopher Erasmus also enjoyed the city's pleasant atmosphere, and Pieter Bruegel the Elder came to Brussels to paint his marvellous studies of life in the Low Countries. Brussels' thriving trade in luxury goods at this time was enhanced by the vogue of its lace-makers and the exper-tise of its highly prized gunsmiths.

The *Ommegang*, or 'walk-around', the most spectacular of Brussels' festivities, gave the resident Renaissance nobility and gentry a chance to show off their riches in a procession around the city. Originally a religious celebration of a miraculous statue of the Virgin (brought to the city in 1348), it soon became an undisguised assertion of the nobility's civic authority. The *Ommegang* is still held every year in early July in the Grand-Place. It was at the event, in 1549, when Charles V introduced his son from Spain to the citizens of Brussels; in 1555, Charles abdicated in his son's favour. The Belgians viewed the new King Philip II with suspicion.

INQUISITIONS, SHELLS AND BEHEADINGS

During Charles' reign, Calvinists had arrived in Brussels, and the people of the Low Countries embraced the Reformation with enthusiasm. Soon, the spiritual rebellion against Catholicism became identified with the nationalist rebellion against Spanish rule, and discontent grew. Charles only dimly perceived the seriousness of this threat to Spanish power and was lax in enforcing his powers. However, Philip, who disliked his northern subjects, was less easygoing. He brought in the inquisitors and surrounded himself with Spanish soldiers, and blood began to flow.

Nationalist resistance was led by William of Nassau, Prince of Orange. Philip, who in 1559 headed back to Spain, sent the Duke of Alba – the 'bloody duke' – to quash the revolt. Two leading landowners, counts Egmont and Hornes, more nationalists than rebels, were executed in the Grand-Place in 1568. However, the Prince of Orange was able to drive out the Spanish in 1576, whereupon Brussels

Count Egmont

Count Egmont is remembered not just through the famous statue of him and Hornes on place du Petit-Sablon, but also through a play written by Goethe and an overture, *Egmont*, by Beethoven (opus 84).

enacted ferocious anti-Catholic legislation. In 1581 the Catholic religion was simply 'abolished'.

This outraged Philip, who sent a large army, under the command of Alexander Farnese, to re-occupy the city. The southern provinces of the Low Countries returned to Spain and Catholicism, but the northern provinces (now the Netherlands) succeeded in breaking away and remained largely

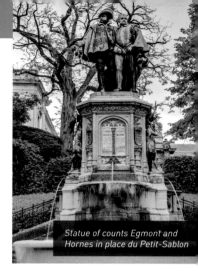

Statue of counts Egmont and Hornes in place du Petit-Sablon

Protestant. Brussels saw a flood of Jesuits, monks and nuns to reinforce the Catholic Counter-Reformation.

Under the rule of Philip's daughter, Archduchess Isabella, and her husband, Archduke Albert of Austria, Brussels returned to a general semblance of order (1599–1633). Life in the capital became quite fashionable, with a constant flow of ambassadors, generals, bishops and cardinals bringing a new cosmopolitan air to the court of the governors-general around the Sablon quarter. The spirit of the age found great artistic expression in the sumptuous contours of Flemish Baroque, which reached its peak with the magnificent paintings of Peter Paul Rubens.

At this time, Brussels was a haven for political exiles—Marie de Medici, Christina of Sweden, the dukes of Bouillon and Vendôme and the sons of Charles I of England. However, by the end of the century it was not quite so safe. In 1695

Louis XIV of France took his revenge for the Dutch and English shelling of his coastal towns with the wanton bombardment of Brussels. Marshal de Villeroy's army of 70,000 men occupied Anderlecht and set up its cannons at the gate of Ninove. For two days, shells and cannonballs fell on some 4,000 buildings, killing 1,000 people, yet the city did not surrender. The Grand-Place was badly damaged, yet the Town Hall's superb belltower survived.

REVOLUTION TO REVOLUTION

In 1701 a dynastic wrangle brought war in Europe, and in the peace that followed, control of the southern Low Countries passed to the Austrian Habsburgs. The subsequent period of growth in Belgium was subsidised by trade links controlled by Vienna. Emperor Joseph II ruled Belgium in the last part of the 18th century with a form of enlightened despotism. His religious reforms and judicial liberalisation upset the conservative Belgians, and the centralised Vienna-controlled administration jarred with its habit of local autonomy, and nowhere more so than in Brussels.

This was at a time when the Americans had thrown off the British yoke, and the French were getting rid of their royal one. In January 1790 the old patrician families of Brussels staged a revolt, which drove the Austrians out and restored their ancient privileges under the 'Etats Belges Unis' (United Belgian States). The revolutionary regime was short-lived: in December, the Austrians returned, only to be ousted in 1792 by the French Revolutionary army. In 1793 the French decided simply to annex Belgium. Their influence was mixed. Increased trade with France brought more affluence, but museums and libraries were pillaged, and many able-bodied men were press-ganged into the Revolutionary army.

In the winter of 1813–14, Brussels saw the French troops depart, only for them to be replaced by Russians, Prussians, Dutch and, finally, by the British, waiting for orders to go into battle with Napoleon in 1815. The rendezvous was around 20km (12 miles) away, at Waterloo, on 18 June.

Napoleon's defeat and the resulting Congress of Vienna brought 16 years of Dutch rule to Belgium, resurrecting old tensions

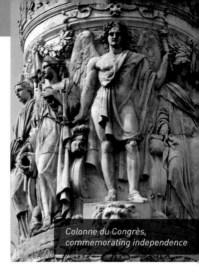

Colonne du Congrès, commemorating independence

and creating new ones. During Napoleon's rule, the national language was French. Even in Flanders, French was the language of the nobility and bourgeoisie. King William of Orange introduced Dutch, previously spoken only by the lower ranks of society, into schools, municipal government and courts. French-speaking teachers were upset by the imposition of Dutch and taught the sciences in Latin. Catholics were upset by the removal of schools from church control, and liberals were upset by press censorship.

INDEPENDENCE AT LAST

With Paris overthrowing its monarch in July 1830, revolt was in the air. In August liberal journalists were active in Brussels, and workers were demonstrating against low pay and poor living conditions. At a performance of Daniel Auber's opera *La Muette de Portici* on 25 August, the rousing aria *Amour Sacré de la Patrie* (Sacred Love of the Fatherland) raised the blood of the bourgeois audience. Belgians of all classes came out on to the streets in a series of civil disturbances. Rioters attacked the Palais de Justice, and sacked the homes of government ministers, while the police and army stood by. In September, King William sent troops to Brussels, and there were many casualties on both sides; when Belgium's independence was recognised on 21 July 1831, the keys of the capital were handed over to the country's new king, Leopold of Saxe-Coburg.

With independence came high economic growth but also social, political and religious conflicts. Tensions were high between Catholics and liberals, and between Flemings (Dutch-speaking Belgians in the north) and Walloons (French-speaking Belgians in the south). Conservative Catholic provinces resisted universal suffrage and so maintained control over the government. This fuelled their fight with the liberals of the capital over education and church power. Although Brussels was nominally bilingual, French was increasingly dominant in business and state administration. The Flemings campaigned with increasing indignation for greater use of their language in the universities and law courts.

Leopold II

Throughout the 19th century and particularly during the reign of Leopold II (1865–1909), industrial expansion and imperial adventures in Africa, particularly in the Congo, brought great prosperity to Brussels. There was a flurry of construction, with mansions and commercial buildings rising up along the wide avenues and boulevards. As ever, the products of the luxury industries – textiles, furniture, lace, fine porcelain, paper and books – were at a premium.

Brussels was once again a refuge for political exiles, notably from Poland, Italy, France and Russia. Germany's Friedrich Engels and Karl Marx organised the socialist German Workers' Club at Le Cygne on the Grand-Place. The two wrote the *Communist Manifesto* here, and then were kicked out of Belgium in 1848, when it was feared that their writings and ideas might reproduce the latest Paris Revolution. There was also an explosion of artistic achievement in the capital. Painters including James Ensor, Félicien Rops and Fernand Khnopff came together in the Groupe des XX in 1883. Brussels was also a major centre of Art Nouveau architecture under the leadership of both Victor Horta and Paul Hankar.

WORLD WARS AND INTERNATIONAL LEADERSHIP

Belgium's historic vulnerability to invasion was displayed again in August 1914, when Kaiser Wilhelm's German armies occupied Brussels. The capital put up a heroic passive resistance, and when the Germans were defeated, Belgium expressed its new-found sense of national unity in the introduction of universal suffrage, the right to strike, a Flemish university and, finally, a truce in the church-school conflict. In the 1930s there was the emergence in Brussels, as in other European capitals, of new fascist groups drawing on social discontent and primitive chauvinism. The fascist leader Léon Degrelle achieved that which had eluded other Belgian leaders: he united Catholics, liberals and socialists in a combined effort to defeat him, resoundingly, in the 1937 elections. These grim times offered the best breeding ground for a flight into the Surrealist art of René Magritte and Paul Delvaux, and the comic-strip escapism of Hergé's *Tintin*.

Then came World War II and another German occupation. The Nazis found collaborators to prepare Belgium for integration into the Reich, and Flemish and Walloon volunteers for separate *Waffen-SS* formations. King Leopold III's passive acceptance of the invasion caused controversy.

After the war Belgium held a referendum in which King Leopold gained a majority of 58 percent. However, not having a majority in each province, he refused to be reinstated and was succeeded in 1951 by his son Baudouin, who proved an immensely popular monarch with both Flemings and Walloons, and the glue that held the country together. Meanwhile, somewhat ironically given its own internal strife, Belgium took on a new role as the capital of a more unified Western Europe and of the Atlantic alliance. In 1957 the EEC (now the EU) established its headquarters in Brussels. The following year the city staged a very successful World's Fair based on the theme of building a better world for mankind, and in 1960 Belgium divested itself of its African colonies.

NATO moved its headquarters to Brussels in 1967, and the city subsequently attracted around a quarter of a million foreign residents to work in military and multinational organisations. In the 1980s and 1990s, the Belgian government introduced regional government to allow greater local decision-making. Today, with the EU having expanded up to the borders of the old Soviet Union, the city's role as the focal point for the continent continues to develop.

HISTORICAL LANDMARKS

AD 979 Founding of the city with the building of a fortress.

1047 Construction of the first city wall.

1303 Uprising of craftsmen demanding greater say in city government.

1406 Dukes of Burgundy take control of Brussels.

1515 The future emperor Charles V becomes Archduke of Brabant.

1531 Brussels becomes the capital of the Spanish Netherlands.

1555 Charles V abdicates. Brussels is subject to Philip II of Spain.

1568 Belgian counts Egmont and Hornes beheaded for high treason.

1576 Under the Prince of Orange, Brussels revolts and drives out the Spanish, but the latter re-occupy the city in 1585.

1695 Louis XIV of France bombards Brussels.

1713 The Treaty of Utrecht: Brussels becomes subject to Austria.

1794 Belgium is annexed by France.

1815 The French are defeated at Waterloo. Congress of Vienna cedes Belgium to the Netherlands; William of Orange is crowned.

1830 Belgian Revolution begins in Brussels, leading to independence.

1831 Leopold of Saxe-Coburg is made first king of the Belgians.

1914–18 World War I: most of Belgium is occupied by German army.

1940–5 World War II: Belgium is again occupied by Germany.

1951 King Leopold III abdicates in favour of his son, Baudouin.

1957 The EEC (European Union) makes its headquarters in Brussels.

1967 NATO's headquarters are moved to Brussels.

1993 King Baudouin is succeeded by Albert II.

1994 Brussels-Capital becomes one of three federal regions in Belgium.

1995 Brabant province, surrounding Brussels, separates into Dutch-speaking Flemish Brabant and French-speaking Walloon Brabant.

2002 The euro replaces the Belgian franc as the national currency.

2013 King Albert II abdicates in favour of his son, Philippe (born 1960).

2014 The separatist Flemish N-VA party wins the parliamentary elections.

2016 Three coordinated suicide bombings in Brussels kill 32 and injure around 300 civilians.

2018 Belgium's national football team finishes third in the World Cup.

Parc du Cinquantenaire

WHERE TO GO

The city of Brussels is made up of 19 *communes* or districts, each with its own council, administration and police force. Every *commune* has a distinctive character based on its history, major industry and social make-up. The central *commune* is the only one called Brussels, but most people travelling to the city know the metropolitan conurbation as a whole by this name.

A well-organised, integrated and inexpensive public transport system makes the greater Brussels area easy to explore. Central Brussels is compact and, with comfortable footwear, is a good destination for walking.

This guide divides the city into a number of easy-to-follow sections, taking central Brussels first and then exploring the highlights of the surrounding *communes*, as well as the battlefield at Waterloo, 15km (9 miles) from the city. We also include excursions to the cities of Antwerp, Bruges and Ghent.

THE HEART OF THE CITY

In the Middle Ages, Brussels was surrounded by a protective wall, with access through seven gates. Inside the wall is an area of 3km by 2km (2 miles by 1.5 miles), a network of narrow cobbled streets, with the Coudenberg hill marking the city's highest point. When Napoleon Bonaparte took control of Brussels in 1799, he decided to tear down the wall and create wide boulevards around the city. These still exist today as the *petite ceinture* or inner ring road, a four- to six-lane highway. It is the *petite ceinture* that, for the most part, creates the boundary between the commune of Brussels and the surrounding *communes* of the city.

THE GRAND-PLACE

There are some places in the world where no matter how wonderful you hear they are, nothing prepares you for seeing them. The **Grand-Place ❶** is one such place. The beauty is almost overwhelming, the skill of the masons awe-inspiring. Yet the square also has a very human quality, with numerous cafés where you can sit and watch the world go by.

The Grand-Place has long been the heart of the city. Its Dutch name, Grote Markt, indicates that it was developed as the main marketplace. This part of town became Brussels' commercial heartland at the end of the first millennium, when nearby marshes were drained, creating land for building.

Markets grew up haphazardly, but towards the end of the 13th century, it was clear that a large open area would have to be planned, and houses were demolished to create the space. The foundation stone of the Hôtel de Ville (Town Hall) was laid in 1401 and soon powerful corporations began building their guild houses close to this symbol of secular power.

These buildings were already some 200 years old when the League of Augsburg – an alliance between the United Provinces (Holland), Britain, Spain and Germany – went to war with the French under Louis XIV, the Sun King. In 1695, Louis ordered the bombardment of Brussels. On 13 August, 70,000 men laid siege to the city's walls, and cannonballs

Two languages

In bilingual Brussels, street and building names appear in both French and Dutch. For simplicity, in this book we have used only the French names (French is spoken by 90 percent of the population as a first or second language). For Flanders, where the Dutch language prevails, we have followed the local practice in citing place names.

The Maison du Roi fronts one corner of the Grand-Place

began to rain down, devastating the Grand-Place. Only the spire of the Hôtel de Ville and the facades of three houses remained intact.

In the aftermath of this devastation, the town council decided that a new Grand-Place would be planned and controlled. It approved or vetoed the design of each house fronting the square, resulting in the Grand-Place we see today.

The Hôtel de Ville

The **Hôtel de Ville** (Town Hall; guided tours in English: Apr–Sept Sun 10am and 2pm, and year-round Wed 3pm) is a magnificent building, whose construction sent an important message about the power that ruled Brussels at the time. While other communities were concentrating their efforts on erecting grand religious buildings, the leaders of Brussels chose to celebrate the civic side of life. The design is an amalgam of covered market and fortified mansion, and each facade was rebuilt to the

Flowers & festivals

Between March and October, the Grand-Place is the location of a flower market (Tue–Sun). It is also the venue of many Brussels festivals, such as the annual Burgundian Ommegang parade in July, when the city's guilds and corporations come together to celebrate their illustrious histories.

original plans following the bombardment of 1695. The 96m (312ft) tower, dating from the 1450s, replaced an earlier belfry. A statue of the Archangel Michael, the city's patron, tops the tower. A series of first-floor galleries and arcades brings coherence to these two separate elements. The Lion Staircase, which now forms the main entrance, was added later (the lion statues in 1770). The coving around the portal features sculptures of eight prophets, while the friezes between the first and second floors depict leading ducal luminaries.

The interior is equally attractive. The highly decorated meeting hall is still home to the council of the *commune*, while the court room is now used for weddings. One wall of the David and Bathsheba Room is filled with a 1520 tapestry showing Bathsheba at the fountain. Walls in corridors and halls pay tribute in sculpture and paintings to the guildsmen who brought the town prosperity, and the royal families who brought it power. A branch of the Brussels tourist office is on the ground floor.

Houses of the dukes and guilds

Travelling from the Hôtel de Ville in a clockwise direction around the Grand-Place, the first highlight is No. 7, **Le Renard** (meaning 'the fox', in French), or House of the Haberdashers, built in 1699. The name refers to Marc de Vos (Dutch for fox), one of its architects. It is adorned with statues representing the four continents known at that time, and Justice blindfolded. **Le Cornet**, next door at No. 6, was the boatmen's guild house and has a superb Italianate-Flemish frontage designed by Antoine Pastorana. At No. 5, **La Louve** (1696) is famed for a statue of Romulus and Remus being suckled by a she-wolf *(la louve)*, which gives the house its name. Above this are four statues representing Truth, Falsehood, Peace and Discord. **Le Sac** at No. 4, the House of Coopers and Cabinetmakers, has one of the facades that remained standing after the French bombardment. Much of it dates from the 1640s, although Pastorana added the upper ornamentation. The house takes its name from the frieze of a man taking something out of a *sac* (bag), which can be found above the door. No. 3, **La Brouette** (The Wheelbarrow) was House of the Tallow Merchants, and is now a café (www.taverne-brouette.be). On the corner is **Le Roy d'Espagne** (King of Spain's House), which belonged to the guild of bakers. Its classical lines have been attributed to the architect and sculptor Jean Cosyn, and the octagonal dome that tops it – crowned with a gilded weathervane symbolising Fame – adds elegance to the square. Le Roy d'Espagne is now a famous café (www.roydespagne.be).

Aerial view of the Grand-Place

The northern side of the square, opposite the Hôtel de Ville, is dominated by the large and ornate **Maison du Roi** (King's

House), built on the site of the Bread Market between 1515 and 1536. The rights to this piece of land passed through the dukes of Burgundy to Emperor Charles V (who was also King of Spain), hence the house's name. In the 1870s, Mayor Charles Buls wanted to redesign the house. Architect Pierre-Victor Jamaer retained the Gothic style, adding the flamboyant tower and arcades. Although its facade is not to everyone's taste, you should enjoy the **Musée de la Ville de Bruxelles** (Museum of the City of Brussels; www.museedelavilledebruxelles.be; Tue–Sun 10am–5pm) inside. Its rooms have exhibits relating to the city's urban development and political and social history. It also displays original statuary from the Hôtel de Ville. The art collection includes works by Pieter Bruegel the Elder and Peter Paul Rubens, but the biggest attraction is the display of some 800 ornate costumes worn by that diminutive Brussels mascot, the Manneken-Pis statue (see page 37).

Three narrow guild houses sit beside the Maison du Roi. No. 28, **La Chambrette de l'Amman** (House of the Amman), was the house of the duke's representative on the Town Council in medieval times. The middle house, **Le Pigeon**, was home to Victor Hugo in 1851. **La Chaloupe d'Or** (Golden Longboat, 1697) is easily recognisable; it is topped by a statue of St Boniface. Originally the House of the Tailors, it is also now a restaurant with a lovely interior.

On the eastern side of the square, you will find **La Maison des Ducs de Brabant** (House of the Dukes of Brabant). This facade of harmonious design is in fact six houses and is named for the figures decorating it rather than its former owners.

Three houses lead back towards the Hôtel de Ville. **L'Arbre d'Or** (Golden Tree) at No. 10 is the House of the Brewers – look for gilded emblems of hops and wheat – and has a small museum of Belgian brewing, the **Musée des Brasseurs Belges** (Belgian Brewers' Museum; www.belgianbrewers.be; daily 10am–5pm). A refreshing beer is included in the admission price. **Le Cygne** (The Swan), next door at No. 9, is now one of the best restaurants in the city. Originally, it housed the butcher's guild before becoming a tavern and surrogate home to political theorists Karl Marx and Friedrich Engels. It was here in 1848 that they finalised the *Communist Manifesto*, though they had both made a promise not to become involved in politics when they were offered asylum in Belgium. **L'Etoile** (The Star) completes the vista. This house, the smallest on the square, was knocked down when rue Charles Buls was widened and replaced with a second floor supported by arcades. Below the arcades you'll find a reclining bronze statue of **Everard 't Serclaes**, depicted in the throes of death. He was murdered in 1388 for defending Brussels against powerful ducal enemies. This effigy is considered to bring continued good luck to the people of the city. Rub his arm and the

The Manneken-Pis

nose of his dog to ensure your share of good fortune.

L'ILOT SACRÉ

The Grand-Place is surrounded by a medieval warren of narrow streets. Their names tell of the activities that took place here in days gone by: Marché-aux-Fromages (Cheese Market), Marché-aux-Herbes (Herb and Grass Market) and Marché-aux-Poulets (Chicken Market). This really was the commercial heart of the city. At the beginning of the 19th century, the area was cut by wide boulevards, created when the River Senne was culverted and arcaded (see page 16). The name l'Ilot Sacré or the Sacred Isle was conjured up in the 20th century to protect it from redevelopment.

One street south of Grand-Place is rue Violette, home to the **Musée du Costume et de la Dentelle** (Costume and Lace Museum; www.fashionandlacemuseum.brussels; Tue–Sun 10am–5pm; first Sun of the month free). Two 18th-century brick gabled houses provide the backdrop to a fine collection of Belgian fashions and lace from the 19th century onwards. Further south, at the corner of rue de l'Etuve and rue du Chêne, is Brussels' famous statue, the **Manneken-Pis ❷**.

North of the Grand-Place you can stroll through the **Galeries Royales St-Hubert ❸**. Completed in 1847, this beautiful shopping arcade (in fact three separate, but connected arcades) was one of the first of its kind in Europe; nowadays, it features the best in Brussels' labels. Glass ceilings allow light to flood the walkways. The Galeries intersect rue des Bouchers, a pedestrian-only street peppered with restaurants and one of the most atmospheric places in which to eat on a summer evening.

Taking the western route out of the Grand-Place along rue au Beurre (Butter Street), look out for the Dandoy shop (www.maisondandoy.com) on your left. This family-run business, started in 1829, is a Brussels institution. Stop by for delicious marzipan and *speculoos* biscuits before you start your itinerary, and, in summer, try the refreshing ice cream. At the end of rue au Beurre, you will find the rear facade of the ornate **Bourse** ❹ (Stock Exchange) directly ahead. A relatively recent Brussels monument, it was completed in 1873 on the site of a former convent.

⊙ MANNEKEN-PIS

Why are large crowds always gathered at the corner of rue de l'Etuve and rue du Chêne? There are almost more cameras here than at a Hollywood premiere. This is the site of Manneken-Pis, the irreverent little statue whose method of delivering water to the fountain below embodies the somewhat offbeat attitude of the average native *Bruxellois*.

The tiny chap is renowned for his wardrobe of around 800 suits – the first one was a gift from the Elector of Bavaria in 1698 – though you may find him naked when you visit. He has been kidnapped three times: once in 1745 by the English, and again in 1747 by the French. On the third and last occasion, in 1817, Manneken-Pis was found broken in pieces. In fact, the statue you see today is a replica of one that was fashioned from the fragments.

In a busy part of town, the 11th-century Romanesque **Église St-Nicolas** (Church of St Nicholas; Mon–Fri 8am–6.30pm, Sat 9am–6pm, Sun 9am–7.30pm; free) is a spiritual oasis. Refurbished in Gothic style in the 14th century and rebuilt several times since, the little church still shows traces of its original rough construction.

Place de la Monnaie to Place de Brouckère

To the north of the Bourse is **place de la Monnaie**, where the Belgian Revolution started in 1830 – crowds rushed out of the **Théâtre Royal de la Monnaie ❺** after hearing the opera *La Muette de Portici*. **Place des Martyrs**, just a little way north, commemorates those who died in the fight for independence in 1830. The restored buildings are in the neoclassical style and were constructed in the 1770s, though a number of monuments were added in the 1870s and 1880s. You can reach the square by going along rue Neuve, a busy shopping street.

From place de la Monnaie, it is only a short walk to **place de Brouckère ❻**, created in the late 1800s as a homage to the grand squares of Paris. Mayor Jules Anspach wanted his city to rival the French capital and held a competition to make sure the buildings on the square were the finest possible. Today, many have been replaced by more modern structures and those that remain are somewhat lost in a sea of neon. Place de Brouckère is one of the city's busiest entertainment centres.

The cathedral

The **Cathédrale des Sts-Michel-et-Gudule ❼** (www.cathedralis bruxellensis.be; Mon–Fri 7.30am–6pm, Sat 7.30am–3.30pm, Sun 2–6pm; cathedral free, charge to crypt, treasury and archaeological zone; crypt by appointment only) is a few minutes' walk to the northeast of the Grand-Place. The cathedral was founded as a church in 1047, dedicated to the Archangel Michael. Gudule was a saint from Flanders, and her relics were kept in the chapel at St-Géry until being transferred here. The choir dates from the 13th century, and the nave from the 14th century. The church gained cathedral status in 1962.

The approach to the cathedral has been landscaped, and a flight of steps was added in 1860 to make the most of the views of the 15th-century facade. The twin towers are by Jan van Ruysbroeck, the designer of the Town Hall tower. Stained-glass windows show members of the Burgundian and Spanish ruling families, along with biblical scenes. Above the choir are five windows depicting Louis II and his wife Marie of Habsburg, while the windows of the northern transept show Charles V and his wife Isabella of Portugal. A number of royals, including Charles of Lorraine, are buried in the chancel. The pulpit is perhaps the most ornate element in the cathedral. The depiction of Adam and Eve being driven from the Garden of Eden was carved in 1699 by Hendrik Verbruggen of Antwerp. Below ground are the remains of two towers (c.1200), corners of the original church dating from the 10th century.

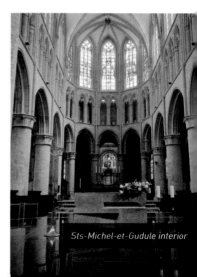

Sts-Michel-et-Gudule interior

Comic Strip Centre

On the northern outskirts of l'Ilot Sacré, on rue des Sables, is a museum commemorating Belgian artists' significant contribution to the development of the comic strip as an art form. The **Centre Belge de la Bande-Dessinée** ❽ (Belgian Comic Strip Centre; www.comicscenter.net; daily 10am–6pm) acts as a resource centre for studies into the genre and has exhibits that bring these comic book and celluloid heroes to life, with *Tintin* and his inventor Hergé taking pride of place. The museum is housed in the Art Nouveau former Waucquez department store, designed and built by Victor Horta in 1906, and faithfully restored.

THE LOWER CITY

West of the Bourse, the Lower City has seen many changes over the last 1,000 years. In the 13th century, a large

Comic Strip Center

community of *béguines* (religious lay women) was established in the Convent of Notre-Dame de la Vigne. The women found safety in the order, living in a large walled compound. The compound was ransacked and abolished during the French Revolution, and now only the **Église St-Jean-Baptiste-au-Béguinage** remains.

> ### Hergé
>
> The actual name of Tintin's creator was Georges Rémi. Hergé is the French pronunciation of his initials rendered in reverse.

Boulevard Anspach separates the Ilot Sacré from the oldest areas of the city, centred on **place St-Géry ❾**. The fine covered market hall (1881; Halles Saint-Géry; www.sintgorikshallen.be) in the square is now a cultural centre, surrounded by lively bars and restaurants.

Following the completion of the Willebroeck Canal between Brussels and Antwerp in 1561, goods could be transported to the city by water. Quays built in what is now the Marché-aux-Poissons (Fish Market) have since been filled in, but the street names still relate to their original purposes: quai aux Briques (bricks) and quai au Bois-à-Brûler (firewood), for example. The most central quay reaches as far as place Ste-Catherine with **Église Ste-Catherine** at its centre. This church originates in the 14th century but was rebuilt in 1854. The square is also the location of the Tour Noire (Black Tower), one of the few remains of the original city wall.

PLACE ROYALE

While the commercial town grew on marshy ground, the powerful families lived on Coudenberg (Cold Hill). Today, this part of town still has palaces, and is home to some of the city's major museums. To reach the museums, walk east from the Grand-Place through the gardens of the **Mont des Arts**, passing the statues of King Albert I and his wife Queen Elisabeth facing each other across place de l'Albertine. The Monts des Arts complex was a contentious redevelopment. It was a project to create a centre of arts and learning backed by Leopold II but resulted in the destruction of a residential area in the 1890s. Unfortunately, before the rebuilding began, Leopold died, and the project foundered. A large garden area was a temporary solution that lasted until after World War II. The building of the **Bibliothèque Royale de Belgique** (Belgian Royal Library; www.kbr.be) in 1954 and the public records office (begun in 1960) have encased the remaining gardens in stone and concrete.

Once through the gardens, there is a view up to **place Royale** ⑩, decorated with a statue of Godefroid de Bouillon, a crusader and ruler of Jerusalem. Behind this you will see the campanile of a grand neoclassical church, the **Église St-Jacques-sur-Coudenberg** . This part of the capital was changed greatly by Charles of Lorraine when he became governor of the Low Countries in the mid-1700s. He looked towards Vienna for inspiration and

Place Ste-Catherine

brought together the then-disparate architectural styles of Coudenberg to create a unified ensemble. The **Musée du XVIIIe Siècle** can be seen in elegant place du Musée in the Louis XVI Palais de Charles de Lorraine (Museum of the Eighteenth Century; the palace is closed for renovation until 2019), though Charles died before it was completed.

Musée des Instruments de Musique

As you walk towards place Royale you'll see a splendid Art Nouveau building on your left. This is the **Old England Department Store**, designed in 1899 by Paul Saintenoy. The building now houses the **Musée des Instruments de Musique** (Musical Instruments Museum; www.mim.be; Tue–Fri 9.30am–5pm, Sat–Sun 10am–5pm). The museum displays over 1,500 musical instruments in 90 groups relating to type and age. On entering, you receive headphones that allow you to listen to a selection of music at each site.

ART MUSEUMS

From place Royale, it is easy to see Charles of Lorraine's vision for the area. Turning right down rue de la Régence, on your immediate right are the **Musées Royaux des Beaux-Arts de Belgique** ⓫ (Royal Museums of Fine Arts of Belgium; www.fine-arts-museum.be; Tue–Fri 10am–5pm; weekends 11am-6pm; first Wed of the month from 1pm; free), including both historical and modern art. This is one of the finest collections in Europe, started at the behest of Napoleon Bonaparte.

The **Musée d'Art Ancien** (Museum of Historical Art) offers more than 1,200 canvasses, with a wealth of Flemish masters on show. Works by Dirk Bouts (1420–75) and Hans Memling (1439–94) showcase the 1400s, with Memling's *La Vierge et l'Enfant* being particularly notable. Hieronymus Bosch (c.1450–1516) and Gerard David (c.1460–1523) lead into the 1500s. Pieter Bruegel (1527–69), whose realism had a profound influence on art within the Low Countries, is also represented, along with Peter Paul Rubens (1577–1640) and his pupil Antony van Dyck (1599–1641). Works by Dutch artists Frans Hals (born in Antwerp) and Rembrandt are featured, too. In addition, the museum devotes space to the artistic

When the flag flies over the Palais Royal, the king is in residence

movements that developed at the end of the 19th century, such as Impressionism – the collection includes paintings by Renoir, Monet and Sisley. On the south side of the museum is a small sculpture garden.

The **Musée d'Art Moderne** (Modern Art Museum) concentrates on pieces from the late 19th century onwards. Though you enter through a neoclassical building, part of the museum is, in fact, built below ground level with a huge central glass wall allowing light into the galleries. Cubist, Fauvist, Abstract and Surrealist artists are represented. The pieces are arranged chronologically and feature Belgian artists such as Rik Wouters (1882–1916) and Paul Delvaux (1897–1994), along with work by Picasso, Dalí, Miró, Gauguin and Seurat.

In 2009, the Hôtel Altenloh, a mansion from 1779, became home to the **Musée Magritte** (www.musee-magritte-museum. be; Tue–Sun 10am–5pm; first Wed of the month free from 1pm). The museum showcases a large collection of works by the Belgian surrealist artist René Magritte (1898–1967).

Sandwiched between the Magritte galleries and the Museum of Historical Art is the Musée Fin-de-Siècle (rue de la Régence 3; www.fin-de-siecle-museum.be; Tue–Sun 10am–5pm; first Wed of the month free from 1pm), which displays works from the turn of the 19th and 20th centuries, including Art Nouveau furniture and decorative pieces.

PARC DE BRUXELLES AND PALAIS ROYAL

If you head north from the museum entrance back across place Royale, you will see ahead the trees of the **Parc de Bruxelles** ⑫. Originally a hunting preserve of the dukes of Brabant, it has been open land for several centuries. The formal park with ornamental fountains and statuary in the French style was completed in 1835.

On its south side, the garden looks on to the impressive front facade of the **Palais Royal** ⓭ (Royal Palace), once part of the site of the Palace of the Dukes of Brabant. Construction began in 1820 following a fire, which destroyed the previous building. It was greatly modified under Leopold II during his reign (1865–1909), with several of the chambers and the facade given Classical and Louis XVI-style embellishments. The palace is now used for ceremonial occasions, as the royal family lives at Laeken Palace on the northern outskirts of the city. If the king is in residence, you will see the Belgian flag fluttering on the flagpole above the entrance.

The palace is open for tours from the end of July to the beginning of September, but if you want to know more about the Belgian royal family, visit the **Musée BELvue** (www.belvue.be; Tue–Fri 9.30am–5pm, Sat–Sun 10am–6pm), which is housed in the Bellevue Apartments in the east wing of the palace. The rooms still retain their original splendour. Tasteful exhibits have been added to tell the story of each royal reign in chronological order, including both the personal and professional lives of the monarchs. Artefacts include personal belongings and photographs of the royal family. There is also a memorial to King Baudouin (see page 26), who died in 1993.

On the opposite side of the Parc de Bruxelles is the **Palais de la Nation**, which was constructed in 1783. It has been the seat of the Belgian government since 1830.

Congress Column

The Colonne du Congrès (Congress Column), on rue Royale, commemorates Belgium's Independence Revolution in 1830. Atop its 47m (153ft) shaft stands a statue of King Leopold I (1790–1865). At its base is the Tomb of the Unknown Soldier.

Travel back towards the old part of the city via rue Baron Horta and you will find **BOZAR/Palais des Beaux-Arts** (Centre for Fine Arts; www.bozar.be; exhibitions in the Palace: Tue–Sun 10am–5.30pm, Thu until 8.30pm) on the corner to your left, on rue Ravenstein. Completed in 1928 to a design by Victor Horta, it is greatly admired for its interior detail. Major cultural events such as the Queen Elisabeth Music

Guild statue in place du Petit-Sablon

Contests are held here; temporary exhibitions take place in the foyer, so something is always happening. Also on rue Baron Horta, the **Cinematek** (www.cinematek.be; daily, times vary), an art-house cinema, has daily screenings.

LE SABLON

Once a marshy wasteland, this part of Brussels saw mansions built for the ruling families in the 16th century, but became especially fashionable in the 19th century. Many fine town houses date from this time. Today, it has numerous antiques shops, art galleries, good restaurants and busy bars, which makes it a popular place to browse and have lunch.

It is easy to find the Sablon from the Museé des Beaux-Arts area. A short walk south along rue de la Régence brings you to the **Église Notre-Dame du Sablon** (Church of Our Blessed Lady of the Sablon; Mon–Fri 9am–5pm, Sat–Sun 10am–6.30pm; free) at the top of **place du Grand-Sablon** . The church was built in 1304 by the guild of crossbowmen, and the statue of Our Lady here is said to have healing properties. The church has undergone several extensions and embellishments, the last in the 19th century. Since the 15th century, the square in the shadow of the church has hosted markets. It is still home to an antiques market every weekend.

Behind the church and across rue de la Régence is **place du Petit-Sablon** , with its own park, laid out in 1890. It is decorated with historically significant statuary. Each post of the wrought-iron fence around the park is topped with the bronze figure of a man portraying a trade guild. Pride of place within the park is taken by a large sculptured tribute to counts Hornes and Egmont, who were beheaded in the Grand-Place in 1568 following unsuccessful protests against the excesses of Spanish rule. Beyond the square you'll see the **Palais d'Egmont** (1534), once the family home of the Dukes of Egmont, but now housing part of the Belgian Ministry of Foreign Affairs. You can't tour the palace, but you can enjoy the gardens.

LES MAROLLES

Les Marolles is a working-class district that grew on trade and labour skills – coopering and blacksmithing, primarily. The Marolles has never been gentrified (though in recent years this process has been nibbling at its edges) and retains a unique atmosphere, its streets filled with hustle and bustle.

Overlooking the whole area is the **Palais de Justice** , a huge edifice that became a *cause célèbre* when its plans were revealed. It was one of the largest buildings in Europe when it was completed in 1883, and a large piece of the Marolles had to be demolished to make way for it–much to the consternation of the local people. Everything about the building is on a grand scale, including an entrance porch 42m (150ft) in height.

The rest of the Marolles spreads out to the west and is cut by two main streets. **Rue Haute** is the longest street in the Brussels *commune*, and one of the oldest. The artist Pieter Bruegel the Elder lived from 1562 in a house at No. 132 that can be dated from earlier that century. Bruegel and other members of his family are buried in the **Église Notre-Dame de la Chapelle** ⑰ (Mon–Fri 9.30am–4.30pm, Sat 12.30–5pm, Sun 8am–7.30pm; free) at the city end of rue Haute. Consecrated in 1210, the church underwent renovations in 1421 following a fire, and the Baroque belltower was added after the French bombardment of 1695 destroyed an earlier tower. The interior has several fine works, the best being the memorial to Bruegel (the Elder) by his son Jan. At the *petite ceinture* end of rue Haute, you will find the **Porte de Hal**, the last remaining medieval city gate, saved from destruction because it served as a prison. Built in the 14th century, it was radically altered in the 19th century in the faux-medieval fashion of the day – most of the top embellishments date from this time. The lower original walls have a much simpler design.

The second major street of the Marolles is rue Blaes, which is famed for its flea market (Mon–Fri 6am–2pm, Sat–Sun until 3pm) at **place du Jeu-de-Balle ⑱**. You can buy almost anything here, from furniture and clothes to old records. The streets surrounding place du Jeu-de-Balle are dotted with numerous cafés and bars, as well as lots of secondhand stores.

BEYOND THE OLD CITY

There are numerous attractions to visit outside the old town and within the other *communes* of the city. Some can be reached on foot, the rest by public transport.

TO THE EAST

The area directly east of the old town has perhaps seen the most change in the last 50 years. This area is the heart of the European Union administration, with numerous office buildings housing EU departments, support staff and the diplomatic missions and pressure groups aiming to influence the EU's decisions.

The **Parlement Européen ⑲** (European Parliament) building is at l'Espace Léopold. (It is often derisively called the *Caprice des Dieux* by Belgians, because of the building's resemblance to the box in which the cheese of the same name is packed.) Its curved glass roof rising to 70m (228ft) can be seen from all around this district, and there are particularly pretty views from **Parc Léopold** at its eastern side. The high-tech **Parlamentarium** (Willy Brandt Building, rue Wiertz 60; Mon 1–6pm, Tue–Fri 9am–6pm, Sat–Sun

Triumphal arch at Parc du Cinquantenaire

10am–6pm; free) offers visitors the chance to experience the European Parliament in action via a 360-degree digital surround screen. It also features a virtual tour through Europe and the displays on the history of European integration. South of the park you will find the **Muséum des Sciences Naturelles** ⑳ (Natural Sciences Museum; www.sciencesnaturelles.be; Tue–Wed and Fri 9.30am–5pm, Sat–Sun and school holidays 10am–6pm), which aims to enhance understanding of the natural world, and is best known for its dinosaur collection, particularly a group of more than 30 iguanodons found in southern Belgium in 1905. Several have been reconstructed in upright positions, while others are displayed as they were found.

Just a little way further east from the European headquarters is the **Parc du Cinquantenaire** ㉑. When Belgium reached its Golden Jubilee, King Leopold II wanted to celebrate by creating a monument to national pride. He enlisted the help of architect

Cafe Belga on place Flagey

Gédéon Bordiau who planned a grand esplanade, formal gardens and a ceremonial arch, with two wings to house museum and gallery space. However, the project hit snags and was not complete for the celebrations. The monumental arch, which features a large bronze *quadriga* sculpture entitled *Brabant Raising the National Flag*, was completed in 1888, but the complex later caught fire, and one of the wings has been completely rebuilt in a slightly different style. Today the Cinquantenaire complex houses three museums.

The south wing is home to the **Musée du Cinquantenaire** (www.kmkg-mrah.be; Tue–Fri 9.30am–5pm, Sat–Sun 10am–5pm), a collection of art and historical artefacts that ranges from prehistoric times to the present. The Roman and Greek remains are particularly fine, with beautiful mosaics and statuary. Rooms dedicated to earlier Near Eastern civilisation, and ancient Asian and American societies are also impressive. Religious relics, furniture, pottery and jewellery are all of high quality.

In the south hall next door is **Autoworld** (www.autoworld. be; Apr–Sept daily 10am–6pm, Oct–Mar daily until 5pm), a collection of over 450 vehicles. Many early Belgian car makers are represented, with a number of pre-1920 Minerva cars and a 1948 Imperia, the last Belgian car produced before production was swallowed by larger European manufacturers.

Almost every maker is represented, including Rolls-Royce, Studebaker and Mercedes.

The **Musée Royal de l'Armée et d'Histoire Militaire** (Royal Museum of the Armed Forces and Military History; www.klm-mra.be; Tue–Sun 9am–5pm) is in the north wing and hall. One of the largest museums of its kind in the world, it covers 10 centuries of military history. In the 19th-century section are uniforms, arms and the personal effects of soldiers from Belgian units,

⊙ ART NOUVEAU

For all the demolition of architectural gems in recent decades, the tide seems to be turning towards preserving what remains of a remarkable heritage. And despite being the capital of so many other things, Brussels is perhaps proudest of being the 'capital of Art Nouveau', having been bequeathed some of the finest architecture of this exuberant turn-of-the-20th-century style. Property 'developers' and local government connivance have conspired to destroy some buildings, but others remain to dazzle the eye.

The foremost proponent of Art Nouveau, a style typified by naturalistic forms and motifs, was the Brussels architect Victor Horta, some of whose students continued the tradition. Notable examples of the genre are the Solvay Mansion, the cafés De Ultieme Hallucinatie (www.ultiemehallucinatie.be) and Le Falstaff (www.lefalstaff.be), Magasins Waucquez department store (which houses the Belgian Comic Strip Centre, see page 40), the Old England department store (which houses the Museum of Musical Instruments, see page 43), the Tassel House at rue Paul-Emile Jansonstraat 6 and townhouses in square Ambiorix and square Marie-Louise.

including those of Leopold I. The walls are filled with images of uniformed gentlemen and shot-torn battle flags hang from the ceiling. Another section features 14th- and 15th-century artefacts, with suits of armour, swords and shields. There are displays of tanks and other vehicles, and an aircraft section including a Spitfire and Hurricane from World War II.

TO THE SOUTH

Avenue Louise ㉒, leading southeast from the *petite ceinture*, has cafés, restaurants, department stores and *haute couture* boutiques. There are several Art Nouveau homes on the adjacent residential streets, including the **Musée Horta** (Horta Museum; www.hortamuseum.be; Tue–Sun 2–5.30pm) on rue Américaine. The building was designed by Victor Horta as a home and studio. It is considered to be the epitome of Art Nouveau architecture in Brussels.

Travelling to the end of avenue Louise (by tram from the Palais de Justice) leads you to the **Bois de la Cambre**, a park with lakes and pleasant paths for walking. Just before the park is the former Cistercian **Abbaye de la Cambre** (La Cambre Abbey), surrounded by an ornamental garden containing fountains and pools and the 13th-century church of **Notre-Dame de la Cambre**.

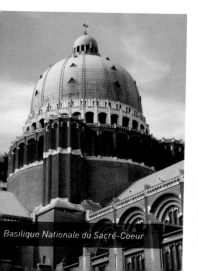

Basilique Nationale du Sacré-Coeur

The abbey buildings now house an art school and the National Geographical Institute. The *bois* itself is, in fact, the manicured tip of the **Forêt de Soignes**, Europe's largest beech forest.

TO THE WEST

West of the heart of Brussels is the *commune* of **Anderlecht**. One of the greatest men of the Renaissance, Desiderius Erasmus (1469–1536), lived here in a house dating in part from 1468. **Maison d'Erasme** (House of Erasmus; Tue–Sun 10am–6pm) is an excellent example of 15th-century architecture and features the desk of the philosopher, a Catholic contemporary of Martin Luther, who railed against the strictures of Catholic dogma. The upper floor has books and manuscripts relating to the humanist movement and religious strife. The Renaissance room is home to paintings by Hieronymus Bosch and Dirk Bouts. Across the street is the **Béguinage d'Anderlecht** (Tue–Sun 10am–noon and 2–5pm), founded in 1252.

TO THE NORTH

Just beyond the *petite ceinture* in the north is the redeveloped Gare du Nord zone, which now has a number of hotels and bars and a lot of nightlife. **Place Rogier ㉓**, home to restaurants, clubs and shopping malls, is the centre of the activity.

About 2km (1 mile) to the west is the huge **Basilique Nationale du Sacré-Coeur** (National Basilica of the Sacred

> ### Beer museum
>
> Situated close to the Béguinage d'Anderlecht, in a family-owned brewery in rue Gheude, the Musée Bruxellois de la Gueuze (Brussels Museum of the Gueuze; www.cantillon.be; Mon–Tue and Thu–Sat 10am–5pm) celebrates traditional Brussels beers. Perfect on a hot summer's day.

Heart; www.basilicakoekelberg.be; Apr–Sept daily 8am–6pm, Oct–Mar daily 8am–5pm; basilica free), in Koekelberg. Begun in 1905 and completed in 1970, this church looks something like a modern take on a Byzantine basilica. The gallery in the dome (charge) affords superb panoramic views.

A short walk east from place Rogier is **Le Botanique** ㉔ (www.botanique.be; exhibitions Wed–Sun noon–8pm), a former botanical garden and glass house of 1826, which was transformed into a cultural centre in the 1980s. The interior is spectacular, with the glass houses – complete with plants – forming a link between the exhibition halls.

Heysel

In 1935 and 1958, Brussels hosted major international exhibitions. The events were held in the north of the city at **Heysel**, where vast exhibition halls were built. Since that time, a number of attractions have developed here. All these can be accessed from the Heysel metro station.

The **Parc des Expositions** is a fine building erected for the 1935 exhibition. However, it is a structure from the 1958 World Fair that captured the hearts of the people and became one of the most popular symbols of Brussels. The **Atomium** ㉕ (www.atomium. be; daily 10am–6pm) was built in the shape of the atomic structure of an iron crystal on a scale of 1:165 billion. Constructed of metal spheres linked by tubes, it was created to symbolise the great advances made in the sciences throughout the 20th century. There is a good view of Brussels and the surrounding countryside from the top sphere, a lofty 102m (332ft) high.

The Atomium is adjacent to **Bruparck**, a large recreational area filled with a variety of activities. Try the **Océade** for water-based relaxation (http://oceade.be; weekdays 10am–6pm, Sat-Sun and school holidays 10am–9pm), observe the sky at the

The Chinese Pavilion at Laeken with a facade from Shanghai

Planetarium (www.planetarium.be; Mon–Fri 9am–5pm, Sat–Sun 10am–5pm) or watch a film at **Kinepolis** (www.kinepolis.be). **Mini-Europe** (www.minieurope.com; mid-Mar–June and Sept daily 9.30am–6pm, July–Aug daily 9.30am–8pm, mid-July–mid-Aug Sat until midnight, Oct–Dec and 1st week Jan 10am–6pm) celebrates European union in a light-hearted way. More than 300 of Europe's best-known landmarks have been recreated here in miniature (1:25 scale). You can visit a 4m (13ft) high Big Ben and a 13m (42ft) high Eiffel Tower – and press a button that causes the miniature Mount Vesuvius to erupt.

The Royal Estate at Laeken

South of Heysel is the **Domaine Royal de Laeken**, a vast estate and palace, where the royal family has residences. Although the palace is not open to the public, the magnificent **Serres Royales** ❷❻ (Royal Glass Houses) can be visited during three weeks in April or May. These were built at the behest of Leopold II following his visit to the Crystal Palace in London and other new glass houses of Europe. A monument to this monarch has been erected in the parc de Laeken opposite the palace. Leopold was enthusiastic about architectural styles and building methods – a passion that resulted in the construction of two Asian-inspired structures to the north of the palace. The **Pavillon Chinois** (Chinese Pavilion), with a carved wooden facade imported from Shanghai, was completed after Leopold's death in 1910. The pavilion now houses Chinese ceramics. The **Tour Japonaise** (Japanese Tower), reached by tunnel from the Chinese Pavilion, was designed and built by Parisian architect Alexandre Marcel. Both pavilions used to host exhibitions of antique Asian ceramics but at the time of writing both were closed for renovation. The nearby former storeroom and workshop for the Chinese Pavilion has been renovated as the **Musée d'Art Japonais** (Museum of Japanese Art), and together the three buildings now constitute the **Musées d'Extrême-Orient** ❷❼ (Museums of the Far East; www.kmkg-mrah.be; closed for renovation until further notice).

In nearby Jette, a house on rue Esseghem was home to René Magritte from 1930 to 1954. The **Musée René Magritte** (www.magrittemuseum.be; Wed–Sun 10am–6pm), not to be confused with the Musée Magritte (see page 58), promotes the Surrealist painter's work.

ENVIRONS OF BRUSSELS

TERVUREN

You can reach the suburban Flemish village of **Tervuren** by taking tram 44 from Montgomery metro station. The route takes you through the commune of **Woluwe-St-Lambert**, a pretty residential

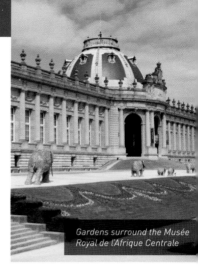

Gardens surround the Musée Royal de l'Afrique Centrale

suburb. It plays host to the **Musée du Transport Urbain Bruxellois** (Brussels Urban Transport Museum; www.trammuseumbrussels.be; Oct–Mar Sat–Sun 1–5pm, other months days and hours vary), directly on the public transport route, for those who enjoy old trams and trolley buses. The Tourist Tramway (Apr–Oct Sat–Sun, depart 10am, return around 2pm) takes passengers on a tour of Brussels on board a 1930s tram. Old trams or buses also run from the museum to the Cinquantenaire in Brussels and the Soignies forest.

Belgian writer Roger Martin du Gard nicknamed Tervuren 'the Versailles of Belgium', and the royal estate here is based on Classical French architectural style and garden design.

In 1897, Leopold II organised a colonial exhibition relating to his expanding lands in the Congo. This proved so successful that a permanent home was built for the exhibits, and an anthropological research centre was instituted. Leopold personally contracted Frenchman Charles Girault, designer of the Petit Palais in Paris, to build the museum. The **Musée Royal de l'Afrique Centrale/Koninklijk Museum voor Midden Afrika** (Royal Museum of Central Africa; www.africamuseum.be; closed for renovation at the time of writing) on Leuvensesteenweg is a stunning building surrounded by acres of formal gardens.

The Lion Mound at Waterloo

The formal gardens surrounding the museum give way to natural forest and parkland. There is a boating lake with lots of bird life, making Tervuren a relaxing spot on a sunny day.

WATERLOO

Of the many battles that have taken place on Belgian soil, the Battle of **Waterloo** ❶ was one of the most important. Its impact on European history was long lasting and it proved to be the final rally for Napoleon in his unsuccessful bid to retake France's leadership. It was during June 1815 that a combined force from Britain, the Low Countries and Prussia began the campaign that would finally destroy the French Emperor. The armies met outside the village of Waterloo on 18 June. By the day's close the French had been routed, and nearly 50,000 men lay dead or wounded on the battlefield.

Travelling to the site today, one can still see how beautiful the countryside must have been. It has changed with the addition of a modern four-lane highway (the Brussels outer ring road). However, many of the historic buildings have been preserved as museums devoted to the battle, the **Waterloo Battlefield** (www.waterloo1815.be; Apr–Sept daily 9.30am–6.30pm, Oct–Mar daily 9.30am–5.30pm). **La Butte de Lion** (Lion Mound), built on the site in 1826 by the government of the Netherlands, marks the spot where their leader, the Prince of Orange, was wounded. The 40m (132ft) mound is topped by a cast iron statue of a lion 4.5m (14ft) in height.

At the base of the mound is a visitors' centre (free), which presents an audio-visual exhibit of the battle, including the tactics and movements of the opposing forces and a time frame. Nearby, in a separate building, is the **Panorama de la Bataille** (Panorama of the Battle), a 110m-by-12m (358ft-by-39ft) circular painting executed by Louis Dumoulin in 1913 and depicting scenes of one of the most important events of the battle. Across the road is the **Musée des Cires** (Waxworks Museum), containing waxworks of

---

◎ BATTLE OF WATERLOO

One of many surprising aspects of the Battle of Waterloo is that it did not take place at Waterloo at all, but in rolling fields 4km (2.5 miles) further south, where the road from Brussels, after passing through the Forêt de Soignes, arrives at a low ridge beyond the farm of Mont Saint-Jean. A traveller taking this route on 18 June 1815 would have run into the French Emperor Napoleon Bonaparte and his 75,000 troops here, doing their headlong best to go in the opposite direction.

More surprising by far is that Napoleon, who won an empire through his supreme grasp of the military art, lost it in the end by putting his head down and charging repeatedly uphill in vain, bloody attempts to shift the Duke of Wellington's 72,000-man army blocking the road to Brussels. 'If my orders are properly executed,' Napoleon told his generals before kicking off the carnage, 'we will sleep tonight in Brussels.' The superb courage of the French soldiers came near to confirming their emperor's prediction. Wellington called the contest 'the nearest run thing you ever saw in your life'.

Diamond city

Antwerp is the world's single most important centre for the diamond trade. Most of the cutting, polishing and trading takes place in the Diamond Quarter, where the offices of the Hoge Raad voor Diamant (Diamond High Council) and the Beurs voor Diamanthandel (Diamond Exchange) are located amid a glittering array of jewellery shops.

the leading military figures involved in the combat.

Strolling around the battlefield, you'll pass the fortified farms of Hougoumont and La Haie-Sainte, which played crucial roles in the battle. At the southern end of the battlefield is the **Dernier Quartier Général de Napoléon** (Napoleon's Last Headquarters), housed in what was the Ferme du Caillou (Caillou Farm), where Napoleon had his headquarters on the eve of the battle. There are a few pieces of memorabilia, including the skeleton of a hussar found at the site.

The British Duke of Wellington had his headquarters at the inn in the village of Waterloo 4km (2.5 miles) to the north. Restored in 1975, it is now home to the **Musée Wellington** (Wellington Museum; www.museewellington.be; Apr–Sept daily 9.30am–6pm, Oct–Mar daily 10am–5pm), which also has a section depicting the history of Waterloo itself. There is a room devoted to the duke, containing numerous personal effects. Other rooms are given over to the Dutch and Prussian armies, and maps of the battlefield.

EXCURSIONS

ANTWERP

Where Brussels has developed into Belgium's most important administrative and legislative city, **Antwerp ❷** (Antwerpen/

Anvers), only 48km (30 miles) to the north, has long been the country's commercial heart. Founded on the River Scheldt (or Schelde), it was an important staging post on the route from England into central Europe and developed into an important trading port by the late Middle Ages. During the Renaissance, Antwerp was one of the cultural capitals of Europe, with the artist Peter Paul Rubens greatly influencing his native town, and philosopher/businessman Christophe Plantin acting as a magnet for advocates of the new sciences.

Walking along the streets of Antwerp today, you quickly become aware of a different atmosphere than that in Brussels. There is a raw energy here, an activity of movement of cargo and goods rather than of paper or files. The city is still one of the largest ports in Europe and the world's centre of the diamond polishing industry.

It is impossible to miss the **Onze-Lieve-Vrouwe-kathedraal** (Cathedral of Our Lady; www.dekathe draal.be; Mon–Fri 10am–5pm, Sat and the day before a religious holiday 10am–3pm, Sun 1–4pm), whose steeple, at 123m (404ft), towers above every other building in the old town. Built during the 14th and 15th centuries, it is a remarkable Gothic creation, the largest in Belgium, and its interior proportions take the breath away. Four

Cathedral of Our Lady

Rubens masterpieces grace the cathedral: *Raising of the Cross* (1610), *Descent from the Cross* (1614), *Resurrection* (1612), and *Ascension of the Virgin* (1626) are colourful and dramatic canvasses that give full rein to the artist's talent. The largest of the cathedral's chapels, St Anthony's, has a lovely stained-glass window, dating from 1503; it depicts King Henry VII of England kneeling with his queen and was created to commemorate a commercial deal made at that time between England and the Low Countries.

A stroll around the outside of the cathedral also reveals a few surprises. The area acted as a commercial centre as well as a religious site and huddling around the base of the structure are buildings as old as the church. These are now cafés, bars and souvenir shops. In front of the cathedral is the small **Handschoenmarkt** with its cafés. Look out for an ornate well, the **Putkevie**, topped by a statue of Brabo, Antwerp's hero.

Walking west towards the river first takes you past the **Vlaeykensgang**, a restored 16th-century courtyard, with an entrance off Oude Koornmarkt. From here, cross over to the **Grote Markt**. This square, like the Grand-Place in Brussels,

⊙ BRABO – ANTWERP'S HERO

Legend tells of how the citizens of Antwerp were being terrorised by an evil giant, Antigoon, who extracted tolls from those who wanted to cross the river. If travellers could not pay, Antigoon would cut off their hands in punishment. Young Silvius Brabo, a Roman soldier, was brave enough to stand up to the monster and beat him, cutting off his hand as a sign of victory and throwing it into the River Scheldt. His heroics not only saved the whole town from tyranny but may also have given the town its name – *hand werpen* (hand-throw).

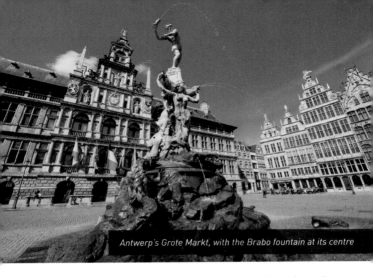

Antwerp's Grote Markt, with the Brabo fountain at its centre

epitomises the power of trade and commerce throughout the history of the city. The mansions that line the Grote Markt were built for the trades' guilds or corporations, which wielded great power during Antwerp's heyday. The most ornate is No. 7, **De Oude Voetboog** (House of the Old Crossbow). At the centre of the Grote Markt is a 19th-century fountain, with a depiction of Brabo wielding the severed hand of the giant Antigoon.

Antwerp's Town Hall

On the square's west side, the **Stadhuis** (Town Hall) was built in the 1560s under Cornelis Floris de Vriendt. It has a sombre balance in its design, with lines of faux columns atop a ground floor of arched doorways. The central section, added in the 19th century, is Flemish in its architectural adornment. Coats of arms of local duchies grace the facade, and a central alcove displays a statute of Our Lady, the protector of the city. Inside, the corridors have dioramas depicting historical council meetings and activities in the chambers. To the south is **Groenplaats**, lined with shops and cafés and sporting a statue of Rubens.

After exploring Grote Markt, head towards the river via the Gothic **Vleeshuis** (Butchers' Hall). Built in the 16th century, it looks like a church with a fine facade and spires, but was a guild house and trading hall. The building now houses the city's museum of music, the **Museum Vleeshuis** (Vleeshouwersstraat 38–40; www.museumvleeshuis.be; Thu–Sun 10am–5pm).

When you reach the river, you can take a boat trip (**Flandria**; www.flandria.nu) downstream to the busy modern harbour. Boat trips leave regularly in summer from the dockside at the **Steen**. This 13th-century castle is the oldest remaining structure in Antwerp, and legend has it that it was the home of Antigoon the giant. It later became a prison, and then until 2008, housed the **Nationaal Scheepvaartmuseum** (National Maritime Museum), which has since moved to the **MAS/Museum aan de Stroom** (Museum in the Stream; www.mas.be; Tue–Sun 10am–5pm, last Thu of the month until 9pm, Apr–Oct Sat–Sun 10am–6pm), downriver at the Bonapartedok harbour.

Printing and art

Walk south of Grote Markt towards the **Plantin-Moretus Museum** (www.museumplantinmoretus.be; Tue–Sun 10am–5pm) in Vrijdagmarkt. Christopher Plantin was one of the most important craftsmen-businessmen of the late Spanish Empire in the Low Countries. His house and neighbouring printing press offer an insight into the man and the philosophy of this time of great expansion and learning, concentrating on writing and printing. Seven antique printing presses are still in working order, and there is a collection of rare manuscripts. Plantin's family sat for portraits that are displayed on the walls; many of the portraits were painted by Rubens.

The **Koninklijk Museum voor Schone Kunsten Antwerpen** (Royal Fine Arts Museum Antwerp; www.kmska.be) on Leopold de Waelplaats is closed for renovation until 2020, but its collection can be seen at other galleries in the city (see website for details). A collection of beautiful art of the Rubens school can be found in **Sint-Pauluskerk** (St Paul's Church; http://

Rubenshuis

topa.be; Apr–Oct daily 2–5pm; free) on Sint-Paulusstraat. The church was part of a Dominican monastery and was constructed during the mid-16th century in the late-Gothic style. The interior is decorated with fine wood panelling surpassed only by the majesty of 15 large canvasses depicting the *Mysteries of the Rosaries*, painted by 11 different master painters.

Rubens House

The **Rubenshuis** (Rubens House; www.rubenshuis.be; Tue–Sun 10am–5pm; last Wed of the month free) at Wapper 9–11, located just off the main shopping street, Meir, is today surrounded by modern shops and cafés, although it still gives an impression of the immense wealth and influence of arguably the best-known Belgian artist. He used the money earned from painting portraits of European royalty to build a large and substantial home for his family – eight children by two wives – and a studio for himself in 1610. The family lived in a Flemish-style wing of the house. It is austerely furnished, but look out for a self-portrait of the artist hanging in the dining room. Contrast this family wing with the studio, which was decorated in the then-fashionable Baroque style. Here you will find Rubens' extensive collection of Greek and Roman sculpture.

Rubens had a hand in the design and adornment of the 17th-century **Sint-Carolus Borromeuskerk** (St Charles Borromeo Church; www.carolusborromeus.be; Mon–Sat 10am–12.30pm and 2–5pm; Sun masses only; church free, Lace Room, 10am–noon and 2–4pm), in Hendrik Conscienceplein, east of the Grote Markt. The artist, along with members of his family, is buried in the 16th-century **Sint-Jacobskerk** (St James's Church; http://topa.be), in nearby Lange Nieuwstraat, inside which there are a number of his paintings, and a portrait of Rubens.

Works by Rubens are also in evidence in the **Mayer Van den Bergh Museum** (Tue–Sun 10am–5pm; www.mayervandenbergh.be) on Lange Gasthuisstraat, and although Pieter Bruegel was a resident of Brussels, there are several of his works here, including his earliest known painting, *Twelve Proverbs*, and his sombre view of war *Dulle Griet* (Mad Meg). The museum is based on the collection of Sir Fritz van den Bergh and includes a large collection of sculpture, tapestries and ceramics from the 12th to the 18th centuries, in addition to a wide range of art.

MUSEUM OF MODERN ART

Known as M HKA, the **Museum voor Hedendaagse Kunst Antwerpen** (Antwerp Museum of Modern Art; www.muhka.be; Tue–Sun 11am–6pm, Thu until 9pm) occupies a former warehouse in Antwerp's old port, on Leuvenstraat, close to the Scheldt. Behind the warehouse's original Art Deco facade, a collection of cutting-edge Belgian and international art is expanding to fill the enormous interior.

In the newer part of town (c.19th century) across the ring road, a boulevard skirts the old town. Browse in the modern stores lining Meir, a pedestrian-only area. As Meir becomes Leystraat, the buildings take on a very ornate style, flanking Teniersplein with its statue of the artist David Tenier (a relative of Bruegel). Cross Frankrijklei and walk towards the railway station along Keyserlei. To your left is **De Vlaamse Opera** (Flemish Opera House; https://vlaamseopera.be), which opened in 1907.

Diamonds galore

To the right of Keyserlei is the diamond district where 80 percent of the world's raw diamonds and 50 percent of its cut diamonds are traded. The streets here are filled with jewellery shops selling items from only a few euros to individual pieces worth hundreds of thousands. If you want to know more about this most precious of minerals, head to Diamondland at Appelmansstraat 33a (www.diamondland.be; Mon–Sat 9.30am–5pm). This diamond showroom and polishing house features films and polishing exhibitions about the trade.

Antwerp Station was designed in French Renaissance style and opened in 1905. Its fine dome is reminiscent of a cathedral, and the station's proportions bear testament to the importance of investment in the rail industry at the end of the 19th century.

Beyond the station is **Antwerp Zoo** (www.zooantwerpen. be; daily 10am–dusk), founded in 1843 on 10 hectares (25 acres) of land.

BRUGES

In the Middle Ages this small Flemish city ❸, known as Brugge in Dutch, was one of the most influential in northern Europe, with a thriving economy based on trade with Europe and England. It was the leading city for textile and tapestry production and was a major trading town of the Baltic-based Hanseatic League. Cargoes of wool, furs and spices passed through its port, which was connected to the sea via the Zwin inlet. In 1384, the Burgundian Philip the Good made Bruges the capital of his growing realm, and artists Hans Memling and Jan van

Along the canals

A tour through the canals of Bruges in an open boat is a delightful experience, and the view from this splendid vantage-point is memorable. All boats cover the same route and depart from several landing stages around the centre (Mar–Nov 10am–6pm).

A ride around Bruges

Eyck were at the centre of a royal court that was one of the most splendid in Europe. But the city lost its influence as early as the 15th century. Cheap textiles from England flooded the market, and the Zwin inlet began to silt up. Bruges became land-locked and in time was all but forgotten.

However, it was the sudden loss of prestige and influence that has helped to make Bruges one of Europe's most popular tourist destinations. The town was never redeveloped, and today it still has an almost complete medieval historical area. Most of its canals remain, and a stroll along the narrow streets offers picture-perfect views.

Tours by carriage and boat

Bruges is eminently walkable, but before you start your own exertions take a tour of the streets by horse-drawn carriage or along the small network of canals by boat. If you have

View from Rozenhoedkaai, in Bruges, across to the Belfry

the time, try both, as they offer contrasting experiences in different parts of town.

The Markt

Bruges' two town squares are linked by a short street (Breidelstraat). The **Markt Ⓐ** is larger of the two, and the commercial centre of the town. In the middle of the square stands a 19th-century sculpture, a tribute to Jan Breydel and Pieter de Coninck, the leaders of a 1302 revolt against French overlords. Over on the southeast side of the square stand the **Belfort-Hallen** (Covered Market). The Belfry houses the **Bruggemuseum-Belfort** (www.visitbruges.be/musea; daily 9.30am–6pm). Built in the 13th century, the Belfry was later extended, and the clock was added in the 15th century. Climb to the top, 366 steps and 84m (276ft) up, for a panoramic view. Part of the way up around the steep stairwell, you pass the 47-bell carillon. Inside the Belfry was the town treasury, and such were the riches of the town that they could only be accessed with nine keys. The adjacent 19th-century **Provinciaal Hof** (Provincial Palace) is the seat of the West Flanders provincial government.

The Burg and Town Hall

The **Burg B** is the smaller of the two squares, and the oldest, dating to medieval times. It was named after the original castle of Bruges (which is no longer standing). Each building on the Burg reveals its own beauty and together they make one of the most coherent, sequential architectural statements in Europe. On the south side of the square is the **Stadhuis** (Town Hall), a Gothic masterpiece built from 1376 to 1420. Its ornate facade has a wealth of detail, adorned with statues of the counts of Flanders, family crests and scenes of daily life. Inside, in the **Bruggemuseum-Stadhuis** (www.visitbruges.be/musea; daily 9.30am–5pm), there is even more evidence of civic pride, with guild pennants hanging from the ceiling. The Gothic Hall on the second floor has a magnificent vaulted wooden ceiling decorated with gilt.

To the right of the Stadhuis is the **Landhuis van het Brugse Vrije** (Palace of the Liberty of Bruges). The mansion, which houses the **Brugse**

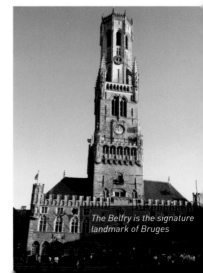

The Belfry is the signature landmark of Bruges

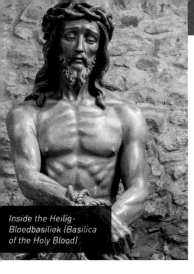

Inside the Heilig-Bloedbasiliek (Basilica of the Holy Blood)

Vrije museum (www.visitbruges.be/musea; daily 9.30am–5pm), is an interesting amalgam of architectural styles. It is renowned for its ornate chimneypiece of marble, alabaster and oak, dating from 1531, in the **Renaissancezaal** (Renaissance Hall). At its centre is a statue of Emperor Charles V, surrounded by other members of the Habsburg dynasty. At the rear of the complex are the remains of a 16th-century building. The facade in front of the square is 18th century. Between the Stadhuis and the Landhuis van het Brugse Vrije is the **Oude Civiele Griffie** (Old Recorder's House), which was completed in 1537.

Basilica of the Holy Blood

West of the Stadhuis is the entrance to the city's most important religious building. This is the **Heilig-Bloedbasiliek** Ⓒ (Basilica of the Holy Blood; www.holyblood.com; daily 9.30am–12.30pm and 2–5.30pm, Nov–March closed Wed; church free, charge for treasury), whose facade was completed in 1534.

Inside, there are two small and richly decorated chapels. The lower chapel is 12th-century Romanesque, while the upper one is 16th-century Gothic in style, with 19th-century alterations. It is in a side room of this upper chapel that the relic that gives the basilica its name is kept. When the Flemish knight and count of Flanders Dirk of Alsace returned in 1150 from the Second Crusade, he is said to have brought back a phial containing a fragment of cloth stained with a drop of Christ's blood. The blood was said to have turned liquid on several occasions, and this was declared miraculous by Pope Clement V, and Bruges became a centre of pilgrimage.

In 1611, the archdukes of Spain presented the church with an ornate silver tabernacle in which the phial is now stored. The phial leaves the side chapel once per year on Ascension Day in May, when it is carried through the streets of Bruges in the Procession of the Holy Blood, one of the most elaborate processions in Belgium. The gold-and-silver reliquary used to transport the phial can be seen in a small treasury just off the chapel.

Opposite the Stadhuis, near the basilica, is the **Proosdij**, formerly the palace of the bishops of Bruges.

Groenerei and Huidenvettersplein

Take the route through the narrow archway between the Stadhuis and the Oude Civiele Griffie. You'll cross one of Bruges' network of canals to **Groenerei** (Green Canal) and see the covered **Vismarkt** (fish market) just ahead. A short walk to the left takes you to the **Pelikaanhuis** (Pelican House), easily identified by the emblem of the bird above the door. Built in 1634 at the point where the canal curves to the right, this was one of many almshouses in the city. There are several boarding points for boat tours along the canal-side here, though you may have to queue.

At the diminutive square of **Huidenvettersplein**, several houses are huddled at the water's edge, with a view of the Belfry rising behind and weeping willows softening the red brick. When the tour boats pass on the canal, you can hardly fail to be enchanted.

Museum of Fine Arts

The street of Dijver runs alongside Groenerei. Here you will find a number of major museums. First is the **Groeningemuseum** ❺, the city's museum of fine arts (www.visitbruges.be/musea; Tue–Sun 9.30am–5pm), which displays a fine collection of Flemish masters including the work of Jan van Eyck, particularly his *Madonna with Canon George Van der Paele*, of Hieronymus Bosch and Gerard David. Works of later Belgian artists such as René Magritte are also on display. Take a walk around the gardens. The whole vista is typically Flemish, with its low-rise, cottage-style white buildings with red tile roofs.

◎ FLEMISH MASTERS

A group of early Flemish artists, based mostly in Bruges and Ghent, have had their work handed down to us under the banner of the Flemish 'Primitives'. The word is used in the sense of primary (being first), and indeed the luminous, revolutionary work of Jan van Eyck (1385–1441), whose *Adoration of the Mystic Lamb* is in Ghent's Bavo's Cathedral, could scarcely be thought of as primitive. Nor can that of his contemporaries Rogier van der Weyden (*c*.1399–1464), Hans Memling (*c*.1430–94) and Petrus Christus (*c*.1410–72), who shared Van Eyck's fondness for realistic portrayals of human and natural subjects.

Later, the focus of Flemish art switched to Antwerp and, to a lesser degree, Brussels. The occasionally gruesome works of Pieter Bruegel the Elder (1525–69), the sensuous paintings of Peter Paul Rubens (1577–1640) and the output of Rubens' students Jacob Jordaens (1593–1678) and Antoon van Dyck (1599–1641) cemented the Flemish connection with the finest art of its day.

The Gruuthuse

In the 18th-century **Arentshuis** (www.visitbruges.be/musea; Tue–Sun 9.30am–5pm) are housed elements of the Groeningemuseum's collection, and an extensive collection of British Arts and Crafts exponent Sir Frank Brangwyn, who was born in Bruges and bequeathed his work and collection to the city when he died in 1956. As a student of William Morris, Brangwyn is an important link to later artistic movements.

An adjacent palace once belonged to a powerful Burgundian-era family, the lords of Gruuthuse, so called because the original owners had the right to tax *'gruut'*, the basic mash of herbs and spices used in the brewing process. Erected in the 15th century, the palace has twice housed fugitive English kings – Henry IV in 1471, and Charles II in 1656. In the garden (free), a romantic brick bridge crosses one of Bruges' narrower canals, offering yet another picture opportunity. You will also find Rik Poot's modern sculpture, *Four Horsemen of the Apocalypse*, gracing the outer courtyard.

The rooms of the mansion display a wealth of daily articles including furniture and utensils. The huge kitchen is particularly interesting – it looks as if the 15th-century cook has just stepped out of it to do the daily shopping.

At the end of Dijver is the **Onze-Lieve-Vrouwekerk** (Church of Our Lady; Mon–Sat 9.30am–5pm, Sun 1.30–5pm; some parts of church free; charge for museum), an imposing church that has a 122m (400ft) brick tower – the second highest in Belgium, after Antwerp Cathedral's. Inside the church you will find the gilded tombs of duke of Burgundy Charles the Bold and his daughter Mary of Burgundy. Mary's death at the age of 25 brought the Burgundian period of Belgian history to an end. The Church of Our Lady also displays a sculpture of the Madonna and Child by Michelangelo, the only one of his works to be exported from Italy during the artist's lifetime.

Hans Memling Museum

Opposite the entrance to the church, through an archway, is **Sint-Janshospitaal** (St John's Hospital, refurbishment of the permanent exhibition scheduled for 2019). Dating from the 12th century, it is the oldest building in Bruges. It remained in use until the 19th century. In the old hospital church you will find **Memling in Sint-Jan** (www.visitbruges.be/musea; Tue–Sun 9.30am–5pm), which is devoted to the work of the German-born master Hans Memling, who settled in Bruges. Although the collection is not extensive, each piece is particularly fine. Look for the *Mystic Marriage of St Ursula*; the detail of this painting makes it one of Belgium's national treasures.

Walk south down Mariastraat, with its selection of chocolate and lace shops. A left turn at Wijngardstraat leads to the Begijnhof, but before this, look for the small square of Walplein and the brewery **Brouwerij De Halve Maan** ❺ (www.halvemaan.

be; guided tours Apr–Oct daily 11am–4pm, Sat until 5pm, Nov–Mar daily 11am–3pm, Sat until 5pm, Sun until 4pm), which has been in operation in the city since 1546. A tour of the present brewery, opened in 1856, takes around 45 minutes, and ends with a taste of Bruges' own Straffe Hendrik beer.

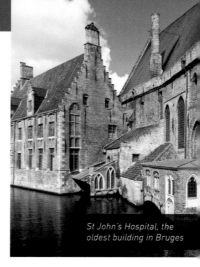
St John's Hospital, the oldest building in Bruges

The Begijnhof

The **Begijnhof** at Bruges (or to give it its full name, the Prinselijk Begijnhof Ten Wijngaerde/Princely Béguinage of the Vineyard) was founded in 1245 by countess of Flanders Margaret of Constantinople and was active in providing security for lost and abandoned women until the 20th century. The circular collection of white painted buildings dating from the 17th century – an oasis of solitude – is now home to a community of the Benedictine order. Just before the main entrance is an open area with a pretty canal and a range of restaurants. The horse-drawn carriages turn around here on their tours. You'll find a water fountain here for them, decorated with a horse's head.

From the fountain, it is only a couple of minutes walk to the **Minnewater** (Lake of Love) and a picturesque park. Minnewater was originally the inner harbour of Bruges, before the outlet to the sea silted up. Today, you can see the 15th-century gunpowder house and scant remains of a protective wall. The open water is a haven for birds, including swans.

The old quaysides

The main canal that served the centre of the old town entered from the north. Today this terminates at **Jan van Eyckplein**, with a statue of the artist, just a couple of minutes away from the Markt. In the square, you can still find fine buildings lining what were once the busy quaysides of Speigelrei and Spinolarei. The 15th-century **Oud Tolhuis** (Old Toll House) is where taxes on goods entering and leaving the city were collected. Today it is home to the West Flanders Provincial Archives. Nearby is the **Poortersloge** (Burghers' Lodge), a kind of gentlemen's club for the wealthy businessmen of Bruges' golden age.

Located at Balstraat 16, east of the central canal, is the **Kantcentrum** (Lace Centre; www.kantcentrum.com; Mon–Sat 9.30am–5pm), a museum and workshop in the 15th-century Jeruzalemgodshuizen (Jerusalem Almshouses). Fine examples of the craft of lace-making, and demonstrations by lace-makers, can be seen.

Nearby on Peperstraat stands the 15th-century **Jeruzalemkapel** (Chapel of Jerusalem; http://adornes.org; Mon–Sat 10am–5pm), built by the wealthy Adornes merchant family. It was inspired by the Church of the Holy Sepulchre in Jerusalem, which two of the family's members had visited. Farther along Balstraat, you come to the city's folklore museum, the **Volkskundemuseum** (www.visitbruges.be/musea; Tue–Sun 9.30am–5pm), affording a glimpse into life in Bruges in the late 19th and early 20th centuries, before tourism in the city took off.

GHENT

In the 12th century, **Ghent ❹** (Gent in Dutch and Gand in French) was one of the largest cities in Europe, thriving on its trade in textiles and its position at the confluence of the Leie and Scheldt (Schelde) rivers. Today, it is thriving as a modern commercial

Graslei quayside, Ghent

town. Thanks to its university, it has a young population, which gives it a vibrancy not felt in Bruges. Ghent also has many interesting historic attractions to enjoy. Much of the town centre is traffic-free, except for the tram services, which adds to the enjoyment of walking. Perhaps the best place to start your tour is at **Sint-Michielsbrug** Ⓐ (St Michael's Bridge), spanning the River Leie just west of the old town. To the left are the old quaysides of Graslei and Korenlei, and beyond them is the medieval castle, the **Gravensteen**. Three of Ghent's landmarks – Sint-Niklaaskerk, Belfort and Sint-Baafskathedraal – lie ahead.

The Church of St Nicholas

The **Sint-Niklaaskerk** Ⓑ (church of St Nicholas; Mon 2–5pm, Tue–Sun 10am–5pm) was built from the 13th to the 18th centuries and is therefore an amalgam of architectural styles. Beyond the church is the **Belfort** (Belfry; daily 10am–5.30pm), completed in 1380. You can take a lift to the viewing platform 91m (298ft) above the town, for tremendous views.

Around the Belfry is the **Lakenhalle** (Cloth Hall), completed in 1441. Both the Belfort and Lakenhalle are on Emile Braunplein, adjacent to Botermarkt (Butter Market), a major meeting place in centuries gone by. In the 16th century, it was decided to build the new **Stadhuis** (Town Hall) on the north side of the square. Work was halted in 1639 and only recommenced as the 18th century dawned. You will notice that the building has one Renaissance facade facing Botermarkt, a Baroque one opposite Hoogpoort and a Rococo facade on the Poeljemarkt side. In the ornate interior of the **Pacificatiezaal** (Pacification Room) the Pacification of Ghent, a treaty aimed (fruitlessly) at ending the religious wars in the Low Countries, was signed in 1576.

St Bavo's Cathedral

The third spire to be seen from Sint-Michielsbrug belongs to **Sint-Baafs-kathedraal** (St Bavo's Cathedral; cathedral: Apr–Oct Mon–Sat 8.30am–6pm, Sun 10am–6pm, Nov–Mar Mon–Sat 8.30am–5pm, Sun 10am–5pm; cathedral free, admission fee for crypt and *Mystic Lamb* chapel; Apr–Oct 9.30am–5pm, Nov–Mar 10.30am–4pm see page 76). This granite-and-brick building is also a mixture of architectural styles,

St Bavo's Cathedral, Ghent

with a chancel dating from the 14th century, a nave from the 15th century and a transept from the 16th century.

The art inside the cathedral represents some of Belgium's greatest cultural treasures. To the left of the main entrance is a chapel containing what has become known as the *Ghent Altarpiece*, a Jan van Eyck masterpiece called *The Adoration of the Mystic Lamb* (1432). Here, Van Eyck achieved reality through painstaking attention to every detail, breaking away from the medieval stylised form. Other masterpieces include *The Conversion of St Bavo* by Rubens and a work by Frans Pourbus, *Christ Amongst the Doctors*, which has many luminaries of the time painted as onlookers in the crowd.

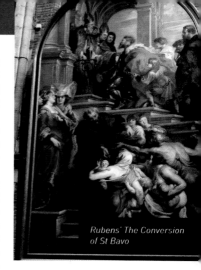

Rubens' *The Conversion of St Bavo*

Korenlei and Graslei

Just to the left of Sint-Michielsbrug, **Korenlei** and **Graslei** once formed the main harbour of Ghent, known as Tussen Bruggen (Between the Bridges). Here you can find some of Ghent's finest old buildings. Both sides of the river are equally beautiful, but on Graslei, look out particularly for the **Gildenhuis van de Vrije Schippers** (House of the Free Boatmen), built in 1531, and Het Spijker (1200), which has been tastefully developed into a bar and eatery. Korenlei rivals its neighbour with the **Gildenhuis van de Onvrije Schippers** (House of the Tied Boatmen), a Baroque masterpiece dating from 1739, and De Zwane, a former brewery of the 16th century.

Gravensteen

Walk north along the river, and as it splits, you will see up ahead the grey walls of the **Gravensteen** **E** (Apr–Oct daily 10am–6pm, Nov–Mar daily 9am–5pm). The outline that the Gravensteen presents is the stuff of fairytales: crenellations and turrets, tiny slits for archers to fire their arrows, and a moat to stop invaders. The castle was the seat of the counts of Flanders and from its construction in 1180 it represented their huge power and wealth. Inside you can visit their living quarters, the torture chamber and dungeons, where grisly instruments are on view.

Just to the west of the Leie, the **Design Museum Gent** **F** (www.designmuseumgent.be; Mon–Tue and Thu–Fri 9.30am–5.30pm, Sat–Sun 10am–6pm) occupies a 1755 mansion with a central courtyard. The rooms display interior design and furnishings up to the 19th century. A separate wing contains modern furniture.

Patershol

Situated behind the Gravensteen, the **Patershol** district is a jumble of narrow medieval streets, dotted with restaurants and cafés. The city's folklore museum, **Het Huis van Alijn** (Alijn House; www. huisvanalijn.be; closed on Wed, Mon–Fri 9am–5pm, Sat–Sun 10am–6pm) is housed in a series of restored almshouses that date from 1363.

Across the canal, **Vrijdagmarkt** **G** still holds its market (Fri 7.30am–1pm, Sat 11am–6.30pm), but visitors arrive to view

Dulle Griet or Mad Meg at other times of the week. This 16-ton cannon stands on the nearby quayside. There are numerous imposing buildings on Vrijdagmarkt. One of the most prominent is Ons Huis (Our House), which dates from 1900.

Gravensteen

Citadelpark
Heading south, on the way to Citadelpark, take in **Sint-Pietersabdij** ❶ (St Peter's Abbey), a former Benedictine monastery now reinvented as a cultural complex. Its two main institutions are the **Kunsthal Sint-Pietersabdij** (St Peter's Abbey Art Gallery; www.sintpietersabdijgent.be; Tue–Sun 10am–6pm), which hosts a changing programme of exhibitions; and a museum of natural history, **De Wereld van Kina** (Kina World; www.dewereldvankina.be; Mon–Fri 9am– 4.30pm, Sun 2–5pm), aimed at children. Also worth visiting is the abbey's impressive 18th-century Baroque church, **Onze-Lieve-Vrouw Sint-Pieters** (Our Lady's at St Peter's).

The **Museum voor Schone Kunsten** ❶ (Museum of Fine Arts; www.mskgent.be; Tue–Fri 9.30am–5.30pm, Sat–Sun 10am–6pm), in Citadelpark, contains works by Frans Hals, Pieter Breugel the Younger, Rubens and Bosch. The **SMAK Stedelijk Museum voor Actuele Kunst** (Museum of Modern Art; www.smak.be; Tue–Fri 9.30am–5.30pm, Sat–Sun 10am– 6pm) opposite offers a diverse collection of Belgian artists.

Galeries Royales St-Hubert

WHAT TO DO

In addition to hundreds of things to see, Brussels also has lots to do, with several important performance venues, a plethora of bars and some delightful shopping opportunities.

SHOPPING

Though there are no 'zones' as such, certain districts do have a greater density of certain speciality shops. The streets around the Grand-Place are filled with shops selling cheap knick-knacks, T-shirts, mugs and keyrings–all the usual budget tourist remembrances but also handmade lace, pralines and crystal. For antiques, head towards the Sablon area, where there are also some excellent art galleries. The weekend antiques market in place du Grand-Sablon is noted for quality items, if not for bargain prices. For bric a brac, head to the flea market at place du Jeu-de-Balle in the Marolles – a veritable treasure trove of memorabilia, furniture, porcelain and glass-ware. For secondhand and rare books, try Galerie Bortier, uphill from the Grand-Place, whose stores have a huge collection.

For haute couture, visit avenue Louise, the nearby Porte de Namur and the several galleries in between, where fine boutiques and department stores are full of the best European and Belgian fashions. For a selection of high fashion in the centre of town, visit the **Galeries Royales St-Hubert** (www.grsh.be), built in the 1840s, where Delvaux has its signature store. For modern fashions, try rue Antoine Dansaert, across from the Bourse. Further out, boulevard de Waterloo has numerous good stores along its length.

High-street fashion and all the best-known European names can be found on rue Neuve, to the north of place de la Monnaie.

Traditional lace items

If it's raining, make for the nearby modern shopping malls of Centre Anspach (www.anspach-brussels. be) and City2 (www.city2. be), the largest in Brussels. Stamps and coins can be found in numerous shops in the narrow streets around rue du Midi, a few blocks south of the Grand-Place.

WHAT TO BUY

With a tradition of trade guilds going back to the Middle Ages, it should not be surprising that Brussels still excels in many crafts. Artistic inspiration takes a number of forms, and as you walk along the city streets, there is sure to be something to catch your eye.

Lace. The women in Brussels' **béguinages** and its ladies of the court spent many hours creating fine lace, which adorned clothing and ceremonial garments. Nowadays, this lace is used to decorate handkerchiefs, napkins, table linens and special items such as christening gowns. Prices vary greatly between machine-produced lace and hand-worked items; knowledge-able sales assistants will help by explaining the different qualities of the pieces on display.

Tapestry. Belgium was renowned for its tapestry-making during the reigns of the Burgundians and the Habsburgs. The enormous tapestries designed for the ruling families incorporated gold and silver thread and were considered so valuable that they were classed as part of the royal treasury. Today, the tradition continues, but, as with lace, much of the tapestry on sale is machine-produced. Handmade work is exquisite but it comes at a high price. You can buy traditional items such as wall coverings or more modern items such as luggage, clothing, or soft home furnishings (cushions and curtains).

Books and antiques. For many years Brussels sat on a major trading route, and it is clear from the range of items available in antique and antiquarian bookshops that goods found their way to Belgium from all across Europe, and later, the colonies. Furniture from England and France sits alongside glass from the Habsburg Empire of Eastern Europe. Prices are steep, but the level of expertise in stores around place du Grand-Sablon is equally high.

Silver and jewellery. Jewellers to the royal court produced beautiful pieces, and today's gold- and silversmiths continue in the same fashion.

Art. Commercial galleries feature the work of established artists and newcomers in a range of genres. You can also buy original cartoon fiches from heroes of the celluloid screen, such as Hergé's **Tintin**. A good starting point is the Belgian Comic Strip Centre in rue des Sables (see page 40).

Stamps and coins. A collection of the world's stamps and coins can be found in small dusty shops around the city. There may be

Lace Society

Belgium has a tradition of making lace – a threadwork of silk, linen or cotton – that stretches back to the 16th century in Flanders. Brussels and Bruges are the principal sales points. Beware of cheap machine-made and imported imitations, unless you want only a simple souvenir. Belgian handmade lace is expensive, but if you like lace this is the only sort worth buying. It should always be purchased from a reputable shop and clearly labelled as having been handmade in Belgium.

something for your collection here, or you can sell or swap your stamps.

Delvaux handbags. These have been at the height of Belgian fashion for many years. Their simple lines and excellent construction have made them very popular among well-heeled, stylish women in Europe.

Edibles. The delightful chocolate and pralines produced in Belgium are available all across town in presentation boxes for you to take home. Dandoy has been producing speculoos biscuits for several generations; you'll find their main shop on rue au Beurre, just off the Grand-Place (www.maisondandoy.com). Alternatively, try Marcolini, on rue des Minimes, in the Sablon district, for hand-produced chocolates (www.marcolini.be). Beer is, of course, another option. With hundreds of different types to choose from, you'll need to do some thorough research before making your choice. Many beer retailers have selections ready for you to take home.

ENTERTAINMENT

With more than 30 venues for the performing arts in the city, there will likely be a wealth of performances taking place, by both local and visiting companies, whatever time of year you visit. The galleries of Brussels host a

Rich and delicious Belgian chocolates galore

huge number of temporary exhibitions of art from around the world. The Visit Brussels website (http://visitbrussels.be) has an extensive section on cultural events in the city. You can also download a free Visit Brussels app to find out what's on.

THEATRE AND MUSIC

When the museums close at night, Brussels takes on a different character. There are several

Antique market, place du Grand-Sablon

prominent theatres around the city, including the **Théâtre Royal de la Monnaie** (place de la Monnaie; tel: 02-229 1211, www.lamonnaie.be), where the seeds of the 'Belgian Revolution' were sown in 1830. It continues to be a major venue, with a programme of opera and ballet. The **Théâtre National de la Communauté Française** (boulevard Emile Jacqmain 111–15; tel: 02-203 4155, www.theatrenational.be) produces strong performances. **Théâtre des Martyrs** (place des Martyrs 22; tel: 02-223 3208, www.theatre desmartyrs.be), is a converted cinema that is home to the Théâtre en Liberté company. The elegant **Théâtre Royal du Parc** (rue de la Loi 3; tel: 02-505 3030, www.theatreduparc.be) puts on mainstream theatre. Modern theatre and dance are at **Théâtre Varia** (rue du Sceptre 78; tel: 02-640 3550, www.varia.be). For a light-hearted view of theatre, try the **Théâtre Royal de Toone** (Impasse Ste Pétronille, rue du

Marché-aux-Herbes 66; tel: 02-513 5486, www.toone.be), a puppet theatre that has been operated by the same family since 1830. They perform classical plays and local folk tales with marionettes.

Classical music venues in Brussels include the glass-houses of **Le Botanique** (rue Royale 236; tel: 02-218 3732, www.botanique.be) and the **Palais des Beaux-Arts** (rue Ravenstein 23; tel: 02-507 8200, www.bozar.be), which is now known as **BOZAR**, and which hosts the Queen Elisabeth Music Competition (held on three out of every four years), as well as numerous concerts. The largest venue is **Forest National** south of the city, with an 8,000-seat capacity (avenue Victor Rousseau 208; tel: 03-400 6970, www.forest-national. be), which stages pop concerts by international names. For

Théâtre Royal de Toone

up-and-coming performers, try the **Ancienne Belgique** (boule
vard Anspach 110; tel: 02-548 2484, www.abconcerts.be).

NIGHTLIFE

Of the three cities featured as excursions in this guide, Antwerp
has by far the most nightlife and entertainment options, followed by Ghent and Bruges, in that order.

Brussels' nightlife scene unfolds in a variety of locations
around the city. Some of the best traditional bars are within
easy walking distance of the Grand-Place. Hip bars and clubs
nestle in the St-Géry and rue Antoine Dansaert areas, and
around place du Châtelain, just off avenue Louise, south of
the city centre. For African rhythms, head to the Matongé
quarter around Porte de Namur. Gay bars and clubs are clus-
tered around rue des Grands Carmes and rue du Marché au
Charbon, close to the Bourse. A slightly older, well-heeled
crowd head to avenue Louise and boulevard de Waterloo.

In the Marolles district, **Bazaar** (rue des Capucins 63;
www.bazaarbrussels.com) is a colourful nightclub that
serves up a variety of dance styles. A perennially hot venue
for techno and house, and with dedicated gay and lesbian
evenings, is **Le Fuse** (rue Blaes 208; www.fuse.be). A location close to the Grand-Place, a commitment to house and
funk, and regular gay evenings are what keep **Le You Night
Club** (rue Duquesnoy 18; www.leyou.be) in the running for
hottest venue in town. The sophisticated **Mirano Continental**
(chaussée de Louvain 38; www.mirano.be) has kept up with
the latest trends over the decades. Hot-blooded types get
to look cool at the **Cartagena Salsa Bar** (rue du Marché au
Charbon 70; www.cartagenasalsabar.be). For a retro disco
party head to **the Nostalgia Club** (rue de la Fourche 49–51;
www.nostalgia-club.be).

In its multitudes of cafés (bars) are where Brussels may be fairly said to live. Among the traditional places that have stood the test of time are **À la Mort Subite** (rue Montagne aux Herbes Potagères; www.alamortsubite.com), **La Fleur en Papier Doré** (rue des Alexiens 55; www.lafleurenpapierdore. be) and **Au Bon Vieux Temps** (impasse St-Michel, rue du Marché aux Herbes 12). All three are close to the Grand-Place. For all its old-fashioned elegance, **Le Corbeau** (rue St-Michel 18; www.lecorbeau.be) has a youthful appeal, especially at weekends, when dancing on the tables is not unheard of. **L'Archiduc** (rue Antoine Dansaert 6; www.archiduc.net) can be almost painfully chic at times, but it puts out some cool jazz at weekends. One of the city's liveliest gay bars is **Chez Maman** (rue des Grands Carmes 7; www.chezmaman. be). **Mappa Mundo** (rue du Pont de la Carpe 26; www.mappa mundo.com) is popular with singles.

FESTIVALS

Brussels holds the **Ommegang** early in July each year, a festival commemorating the time in 1549 when the guilds and Chambers of Rhetoric, as they were called, paraded their pennants before Emperor Charles V. The modern bearers of the head of the guilds dress in costumes of the mid-1500s and carry the banners and pennants of their trades around the Grand-Place (www.ommegang.be). The **Carpet of Flowers** is a biennial celebration held in mid-August in the Grand-Place, when a huge elaborate tapestry of begonias almost fills the square (www.flowercarpet.be).

In Bruges, the **Procession of the Holy Blood** *(Heilig-Bloed-processie)* takes place usually in the latter part of May each year (on Ascension Day, the fifth Thursday after Easter). The most holy relic of the cathedral, said to contain a drop of Christ's blood, is paraded around the city (www.visitbruge.be).

SPORTS

With over 30 sq m (320 sq ft) of green space for each resident of Brussels, and a surrounding landscape without any appreciable hills, it is easy to understand why sports are a big part of the city's life.

Ommegang parade

Cycling. This is a popular sport, though not in the centre of Brussels, where there are a number of deceptive inclines to watch out for (to say nothing of the dangerous traffic conditions). In the suburbs and through the forests there are cycle routes and some urban areas have cycle lanes. It is easy to rent bikes–many railway stations have a bike hire office. Don't forget to wear a cycling helmet.

Football. This is a passion in Belgium, as in most other European countries. Royal Sporting Club d'Anderlecht is one of the most successful teams, with a respectable international history to its credit. For details, contact the stadium at avenue Théo Verbeeck 2, Anderlecht (tel: 02-529 4067, www.rsca.be). The season runs from September to May. The National Stadium (Stade Roi Baudouin) is at Heysel. It holds international games, cup finals, and other national sporting events (tel: 02-474 3940, www.prosportevent.be).

The lake at Tervuren

Horse-riding. The Bois de la Cambre and Forêt de Soignes have bridleways for horse-riding.

Jogging and running. Both are popular, and you are sure to see people taking a turn around the parks. The Brussels Marathon takes place in October.

Leisure centres. Because the weather in Belgium is often inclement, there are many covered sports complexes in Brussels. The Centre Sportif de Woluwe-Saint-Pierre, avenue Salomé 2 (tel: 02-773 1820, www.sportcity-woluwe.be), has squash, outdoor and indoor tennis, a swimming pool, sauna and Turkish bath.

Walking. The leafy Forêt de Soignes is the perfect place for forgetting the city and surrounding yourself with birdsong. There are marked routes for walkers.

Water sports. There's rowing and pedalo rides on local lakes. Visit the lakes at Tervuren, Bois de la Cambre and Forêt de Soignes.

BRUSSELS FOR CHILDREN

At first glance, Brussels may not seem the best place to take children. However, the city reveals some interesting and entertaining things that are bound to keep your children happy. Carriage rides are great fun, allowing children to rise above the sea of heads for a better view. These take place in Brussels, Antwerp and Ghent during the summer, and in Bruges all year round. You can take a canal or river cruise in Antwerp, Bruges and Ghent.

The **Bruparck** complex in the northern Heysel district (boulevard du Centenaire 20; tel: 02-474 8383, www.bruparck. com) has several attractions. **Mini-Europe** (tel: 02-478 0550, www.minieurope.eu) is the 'child-size' attraction, and is both fun and educational. The eruption of Vesuvius is probably the most popular, with its ground-shaking power.

Many of Brussels' museums have attractions that are specifically designed with children in mind. The **Musée des Sciences Naturelles** (Natural Sciences Museum; rue Vautier 29, tel: 02-627 4211, www.naturalsciences.be), with its dinosaurs to enthrall young imaginations, has special activities and workshops for children aged 4–12 years. Covering a subject close to many children's hearts – comic strips – is the **Centre Belge de la Bande-Dessinée** (rue des Sables 20, tel: 02-219 1980, www.comicscenter.net). The **Dynamusée**, Parc du Cinquantenaire 10 (tel: 02-741 7218, www.kmkg-mrah.be) in the **Cinquantenaire** complex offers special activities for children aged 6–12 years, and the **Musée des Instruments de Musique** (Musical Instruments Museum, Montagne de la Cour 2, tel: 02-545 0130, www. mim.be) offers multi-sensory experimentation with sound, along with training courses and workshops. The **Musée des Enfants** (Children's Museum, rue du Bourgmestre 15, tel: 02-640 0107, www.museedesenfants.be) operates a regular programme of sessions involving painting, collage, woodworking and theatre for young children.

Many activities specifically for children are conducted in French and Dutch. For details of programmes in English, contact each organisation directly.

The parks and forests provide perfect environments in which to walk, cycle or ride. The lake at **Tervuren** has boats for hire. If you prefer something more relaxing, take a rug and a picnic and just enjoy the sunshine; don't forget to take some bread to feed the ducks and geese.

If you need a break from the city's sights and sounds, then try **Walibi** (boulevard de l'Europe 100, Wavre, tel: 010-421500, www.walibi.be), situated 19km (12 miles) southeast of Brussels. The huge Walibi theme park has rides with spirals, catapults, river rapids and numerous theme attractions. The attached **Aqualibi** water park has cascades, whirlpools and jungle experiences (tel: 010-4216 03). There are many opportunities for refreshment, so you can spend the whole day here. (To reach the theme park by car, take the E411 and leave at the Brussels Namur exit; by train, take the Ottignies/Louvain-la-Neuve line, get off at Bierges station, which is only 150m/165yds from the park entrance.)

Castles always spark the imagination and the **Gravensteen** (Castle of the Counts, Sint-Veerleplein, tel: 09-266 8500, www.gravensteengent.be) in Ghent is no exception. Images of sword fights on the battlements and prisoners in the dungeons flash through the mind.

A miniature reproduction of the Town Hall in Leuven at Mini-Europe

CALENDAR OF EVENTS

Exact dates of events are subject to change. Check with the Brussels tourist office (see page 130) before planning a trip around one of these events.

February The spectacular Mardi Gras 'Carnival of the Gilles', in Binche, 50km (31 miles) south of Brussels.

April Baroque Spring of the Sablon, classical music performances. The Queen Elisabeth International Music Competition, Brussels.

April–May Royal Greenhouses *(Serres)* at Laeken, in the north of Brussels, open to the public.

May Kunsten festival des Arts: two weeks of dance, theatre and opera performances at venues in Brussels. Procession of the Holy Blood in Bruges. Brussels Jazz Marathon, an international jazz festival with venues around the city. Flanders Festival: classical music events in abbeys, cathedrals and city halls throughout Flanders.

June Brussels open-air music festival in the city's squares and parks. Couleur Café: world music in Brussels.

June–August A daily sound-and-light show in the Grand-Place.

June–October Festival of Wallonia, classical music performances are staged in Wallonia.

July Ommegang procession in the Grand-Place on the first Tuesday and Thursday of the month. Belgium's National Day, 21 July: fireworks at place des Palais. Brosella two-day jazz and folk festival, Brussels. Ghent Festivities, a medieval fair and street entertainment.

July–September The Palais Royal is open to the public.

August Canal Festival, Bruges – every three years (next festival 2021).

9 August Planting of the Maypole, Brussels.

15 August Carpet of Flowers: Every even-numbered year on this day, a flower carpet is laid out on the Grand-Place.

September Antwerp's Liberation Festivities.

October Brussels Marathon.

December Unveiling of Christmas crib and lights in the Grand-Place, and Christmas market and ice-skating rink at the Marché aux Poissons.

EATING OUT

Brussels has no shortage of fine restaurants, and its people enjoy eating out. Belgium does not have to look abroad for good food. It has a fine national and regional cuisine of its own, with hearty dishes based on fresh local ingredients. In addition, chefs have added personal twists to both their own dishes and the national dishes of their neighbours to produce unique creations. There are hundreds of eateries in the city, from formal to informal, with a range of prices, so you should find something to match your taste and budget.

As a cosmopolitan city, Brussels has some excellent international restaurants offering French, Chinese, Vietnamese, Greek, Moroccan and Japanese cuisine, among others. However, if you want to try Belgian cuisine, the information in this chapter will help you through the menu.

Some Brussels restaurants are happy to allow diners' dogs into the dining room, and many let them on to outside terraces. Smoking is not allowed in restaurants, although it is still permitted in some cafés and snack-bars.

WHEN TO EAT

Eating in Brussels means fitting your appetite into set hours. Few restaurants stay open throughout the day. Lunch (déjeuner) is between noon and 2.30pm, while dinner (diner) is usually from 6pm until 10.30 or 11pm.

However, don't worry that you won't be able to eat at all in the afternoon in Brussels. There are numerous informal brasseries and cafés that serve food – though perhaps with a simpler menu – throughout the day. Look out for signs saying 'nonstop' outside an establishment, which simply means what it says.

WHAT TO EAT

There is a wide variety of speciality Belgian dishes, both Flemish and Walloon. Many local dishes are seasonal, so depending on what time of year you travel, you might not see all those mentioned below on the menu. The best restaurants serving Belgian food will change their menus several times each year to take seasonal offerings into account.

A restaurant on rue des Bouchers

Among hors d'œuvres is a beer soup (soupe à la bière) with chicken stock and onions; a cold pâté of veal, pork and rabbit known as potjesvlees; flamiche, a savoury cheese pie with leeks or onions; tomate aux crevettes, tomato filled with shrimp and mayonnaise; and croquettes de crevette, small patties of shrimp. Fine smoked ham (jambon d'Ardenne) from the Ardennes region is also served.

Main Dishes

Belgium specialises in stews. The slow-cooked meat is always tender, the sauce tasty and the vegetables never overcooked. The only 'difficulty' lies in the portions, particularly at the smaller local brasseries, where they tend to be huge.

The best-known main dish is probably waterzooï, chicken (or sometimes fish) stewed with whites of leeks, potatoes, bouillon, cream and egg yolks. Anguille au vert is eel with green herbs, usually sorrel, sage and parsley. Carbonnades

Mussels are a Belgian speciality

flamandes is a dish consisting of lean beef browned in a pan and then cooked in a casserole with lots of onions and beer. *Pavé des brasseurs* is a chateaubriand steak with beer sauce. Oxtail *(queue de boeuf)* is served in a savoury *gueuze* beer sauce. *Hochepot*, a pot-au-feu based on oxtail or pigs' feet, ears and snouts, is another Flemish stew. *Lapin à la flamande* is rabbit marinated in beer and vinegar and braised in onions and prunes. High-quality game usually comes from the Ardennes region, and includes hare *(lièvre)*, venison *(chevreuil)* and pheasant *(faisan)*. If you like ham, try *jamboneau*, a shank of ham cooked with cream and served with potatoes and vegetables. *Boudin rouge* or *noir* is blood sausage, while *boudin blanc* is a lighter version of the same, enlivened by aromatic herbs; all are popular dishes, served with potato purée and an apple compôte.

Vegetables
Vegetable dishes include *chou rouge à la flamande*, red cabbage cooked with apples, onions, red wine and vinegar; and *chicon* (braised endives), often served *gratiné au four* (baked with cheese and ham). In April and May you may find hop flowers *(jets de houblon)* served with poached eggs and *mousseline* sauce. In spring try *asperges de Malines*, white asparagus with

melted butter and crumbled hard-boiled egg, and *choux de Bruxelles* (Brussels sprouts), often with chestnuts and pieces of bacon, and cooked in goose fat.

Seafood

Even the east of Belgium is only a couple of hours from the sea, so seafood plays a prominent role in the national cuisine. Many Belgian towns have a fish market that has been in operation for hundreds of years, and Brussels has long been a big market for retailers and restaurateurs.

Moules (mussels) are probably the most famous Belgian dish. Harvested mostly from nearby Zeeland province in the Netherlands, they are delivered fresh to the capital each morning. Served steaming in a huge bowl, they come with a variety of sauces – *marinières* (white wine and cream), *moutarde* (mustard) and more besides.

One option to try is an assortment of fresh seafood, known as an *assiette de fruits de mer* (seafood platter). These dishes may include anything from mussels *(moules)* and spiny lobster *(langoustines)* to oysters *(huîtres)*, crabs *(crabes)*, whelks *(boulots)*, shrimps *(crevettes)* and sea urchins *(oursins)*. Along rue des Bouchers you can watch your plate take shape as a selection is chosen from the display of seafood on ice nearby. Or you could try a fillet or whole fish, delicately cooked to preserve its freshness. Try salmon *(saumon)*, sole *(sole)*, bream *(daurade)*, mullet *(rouget)* or sea bass *(loup de mer)*.

Desserts

Most restaurants offer cheese as a dessert option. Among as many as 300 different locally produced cheeses are the very strong *remoudou*, the *djotte de Nivelles* and cream cheeses from Brussels.

The local brew

Crêpes (pancakes) are extremely popular and are served with a variety of accompaniments. Try them *aux pommes* (with apples) or *à la grecque*, with icing sugar and powdered spices. Or look out for the two-layered pancake with a tasty cheese filling, known as a *double*. Other desserts include *beignets de Bruxelles* (doughnuts or fritters), *tarte au riz* (rice tart), *manons* (chocolates filled with fresh cream) and *speculoos* (spicy gingerbread biscuits cut into shapes).

Chocolate gateaux take on a spectacular transformation from the ordinary to the divine at the hands of Belgian *chocolatiers*. Belgian chocolates and pralines are exported all over the world, but the best can still be found in Brussels.

Snacks

Waffles *(gaufres)* are the best-known dessert of Belgian origin and these are usually eaten in the street smothered with syrup, or at cafés with a generous helping of chocolate syrup or whipped cream.

If you're looking for a savoury snack, then try the famous *frites* (French fries), available day and night at special stands (*friteries*, or, in Flemish, *frietekotten*) and usually served in paper cones with salt and mayonnaise. *Caricoles* (sea snails) are another street speciality. Eat them piping hot with the spicy

⊙ BELGIAN BEER

Belgium is renowned worldwide for its beer. Historically, the cultivation of hops and barley was under the control of the many local monasteries. This resulted in high standards and differing flavours; indeed one particular type of beer, *gueuze*, can only be produced in a small region of the Senne Valley near Brussels because the micro-organisms that give the beer its distinct flavour are only found there.

Beer in Belgium is treated with the same degree of reverence as fine wine in France. There are numerous small breweries (though many are now owned by larger companies), producing small quantities of beer for the local market. Each is served in its own style of glass either from the bottle as you watch or from the tap, known as *pression*. Some have a high alcohol content. If you are unsure about which to choose, here is a short introduction to the range of beers you will find on your bar list.

Blanche. A cloudy blond beer made from wheat. Low in alcohol and very refreshing, it is a good option for a sightseeing break.

Brune. Darker beer.

Lambic. A beer that ferments spontaneously after exposure to the air. Now only produced by smaller independent breweries (a Belgian speciality). Very yeasty in flavour.

Gueuze. A lambic beer that has been fermented a second time.

Kriek. A lambic beer with the essence of fresh fruit that has been left to develop in huge vats. Cherry is the most popular.

Trappist. This is the strongest beer in Belgium. It is full-flavoured, dark in colour, with a distinctive smell of malt. Trappist beers date from the time of the monasteries and are enjoying a period of renewed popularity today.

broth in which they were cooked. You will also find a full range of sandwiches on offer. The most popular local bread for sandwiches is the *pistolet*, a large, crusty baguette.

Drinks

Coffee – hot, dark and strong – is the local drink of choice by day. If you want it with milk, ask for it *au lait*. Bars always serve coffee, tea and hot chocolate in addition to alcoholic drinks, a full range of international-brand spirits plus soft drinks or sodas. Try the locally made gin, which is known as *pèkèt*.

Most restaurants have a wine list – and some, particularly at the top end of the market, have very good cellars – and will offer you a good-value house wine in addition to more expensive bottles. Brasseries and smaller restaurants also offer house wine in half-litre and litre *pichets* or carafes. These are normally simple, but drinkable wines that pair well with the hearty meals on offer.

TO HELP YOU ORDER...

English **French** *Dutch*

Could we have a table? **Une table, s'il vous plaît?** *Heeft u een tafel voor ons*?

Do you have a set menu? **Avez-vous un menu du jour?** *Heeft u een menu van de dag?*

I'd like a/an/ some... **J'aimerais...** *Ik zou graag hebben...*

beer **une bière** *een pils*

butter **du beurre** *boter*

bread **du pain** *brood*

cheese **du fromage** *kaas*

coffee **un café** *koffie*

egg(s) **un (des) œuf(s)** *een ei (eieren)*

menu **la carte** *een menu*

sugar **du sucre** *suiker*

tea **du thé** *thee*
wine **du vin** *wijn*

...AND READ THE MENU IN FRENCH

agneau lamb
bœuf beef
canard duck
champignons mushrooms
chou cabbage
choufleur cauliflower
crevettes shrimps
épinards spinach
fraises strawberries
haricots verts green beans
jambon ham
lapin rabbit
moules mussels

oie goose
petits pois peas
pommes apples
pommes de terre
    potatoes
porc pork
poulet chicken
pruneaux prunes
raisins grapes
riz rice
rognons kidneys
saucisse sausage
veau veal

...AND IN DUTCH

aardappelen potatoes
aardbeien strawberries
bloemkool cauliflower
druiven grapes
eend duck
forel trout
frieten (fries) French fries
garnalen shrimps
has hare
kaas cheese
kalfskotelet veal chop
karbonade chop
kip chicken

konijn rabbit
mosselen mussels
nieren kidneys
pruimen prunes
rodekool red cabbage
rund beef
spruitjes Brussels
    sprouts
tong sole
uien onions
varkensvlees pork
vis fish
worst sausage

PLACES TO EAT

We have used the following symbols to give an idea of the price for a dinner for one, without wine:

€€€€   over 100 euros
€€€   60–100 euros
€€   30–60 euros
€   below 30 euros

BRUSSELS

Grand-Place/Ilot Sacré/fish market

La Belle Maraîchère €€ *place Ste-Catherine 11a, tel: 02-512 9759,* www.labellemaraichere.com. Seafood delivered fresh from the coast is the speciality at this restaurant. The fishermen's stew is highly regarded. Open Fri–Tue, lunch noon–2.30pm, dinner 6–10pm.

Chez Léon € *rue des Bouchers 18, tel: 02-511 1415,* www.chezleon.be. Mussels are big in Belgium, and nowhere more so than at this mussels specialist near the Grand-Place – something that has been the case since 1893. It's not fancy, and the approach even verges on fast-food, but there's nothing wrong with its mollusc speciality, served in a variety of ways. Open Sun–Thu 11.30am–11pm, Fri–Sat 11.30am–11.30pm.

Comme Chez Soi €€€€ *place Rouppe 22, tel: 02-512 2921,* www.commechezsoi.be. Brussels' top restaurant, just off boulevard Anspach, is styled in Art Nouveau in homage to Victor Horta. Its French and Belgian dishes area delight for the senses. You can eat in the dining room or take one of the tables in the kitchen. It is essential to book several weeks in advance. Open Tue–Wed dinner 7–9pm, Thu–Sat lunch noon–1pm, dinner 7–9pm.

L'Ecailler du Palais Royal €€€ *rue Bodenbroeck 18, tel: 02-512 8751,* www.lecaillerdupalaisroyal.be. This restaurant offers a gastronomic event featuring exquisite seafood, fine wine and impeccable service. Food is served in opulent surrounds – think dark wood and blue velvet. Open Mon–Sat lunch noon–2.30pm, dinner 7–10.30pm.

In 't Spinnekopke €€ *place du Jardin-aux-Fleurs 1, tel: 02-511 8695,* www.spinnekopke.be. Said to be the oldest tavern in Brussels, In 't Spinnekopke serves ample portions of Flemish dishes, which are accompanied by a choice of more than 100 Belgian beers. You'll find it just beyond place St-Géry. Open Mon–Fri, lunch noon–2.30pm, dinner 6.30–11pm; Sat dinner only.

't Kelderke € *Grand-Place 15, tel: 02-513 7344,* www.restaurant-het-kelderke.be. A typical Brussels bar/restaurant hidden away in a cellar room below the Grand-Place. It serves the very best Flemish dishes, all washed down with excellent beer. The place has an informal atmosphere and is always noisy and very busy because it's such good value. Open daily noon–11pm, Fri–Sat until 12am.

La Maison du Cygne €€€ *rue Charles Buls 2, tel: 02-511 8244.* Originally home of the butcher's guild before becoming a tavern frequented by Marx and Engels. The ornate dining room on the second floor has great views over the Grand-Place. Open Tue–Sat, lunch noon–2.30pm, dinner 7–10.30pm, Sat dinner only.

La Manufacture € *rue Notre-Dame du Sommeil 12–20, tel: 02-502 2525,* www.lamanufacture.be. A beacon of good taste in a former designer leather-goods factory in the Lower Town. You dine on French-based world cuisine, amid iron pillars, exposed air ducts, wood floors, leather benches, polished wood and stone tables. On sunny summer days, the shaded outdoor terrace is a pleasant place on which to eat. Open Mon–Fri noon–2pm and 7–10.30pm, Sat 7–11pm.

De l'Ogenblik €€ *galerie des Princes 1, tel: 02-511 6151,* www.ogenblik.be. On the edge of the Galeries Royales St-Hubert, this restaurant combines the simple décor of a chic French brasserie with Belgian service and a Franco-Belgian menu of meat and seafood dishes. Open Mon–Sat, lunch noon–2.30pm, dinner 7pm–midnight.

La Roue d'Or €€ *rue des Chapeliers 26, tel: 02-514 2554,* www2.resto. be/rouedor. This Art Deco brasserie, off the Grand-Place, has murals inspired by René Magritte, a profusion of silver gilt, and a typical Belgian menu, which also includes a few French dishes. Open daily noon–12.30am.

Le Sablon/Les Marolles

Les Caves du Sablon €€€ *rue de Pigeons 9, tel: 02-513 1220,* www.les cavesdusablon.be. An atmospheric cellar restaurant, tucked away along a side street. The small but well crafted menu includes Iberian appetisers and a tasting menu that features innovative dishes such as red tuna with foie gras and eggplant graffiti. There's also a large selection of gin, whisky and rum. Open for dinner 6pm-12am.

Chez Richard € *rue des Minimes 2, tel: 02-479 611 256.* A relaxed meeting place close to the Marolles flea market. The high-quality menu features Belgian and French dishes, including classics such as half-cooked hamburger and delicious "discoveries", such as avocado mousse. Open 8am–1pm, terrace closes at 11pm.

Beyond the Old City

Brugmann €€€ *avenue Brugmann 52-54, tel: 02-880 5554,* www.brug mann.com. Located in a majestic mansion building near Abbe Froidure park, this elegant gourmet restaurant specialises in modern interpretations of traditional cuisine, including twists on French classics. Open daily lunch 12–2.30pm, dinner 7–10.30pm.

Bruneau €€€ *avenue Broustin 73–5, tel: 02-421 7070,* www.bruneau.be. Occupying a nicely decorated town house a little way from the centre, near the National Basilica of the Sacred Heart, has a faithful following for its contemporary and imaginative French cuisine, and outdoor dining in summer. Open Thu–Mon, lunch noon–2.30pm, dinner 7–10pm.

Le Chalet de la Forêt €€€ *drève de Lorraine 43, tel: 02-374 5416,* www.lechaletdelaforet.be. Fine French cuisine is served in the elegant dining room or on the terrace of this restaurant at the edge of the Forêt de Soignes, making it a perfect lunch venue for excursions to the Waterloo battlefield or Tervuren. Open Mon–Fri, lunch noon–2.30pm, dinner 7–10pm.

Upper City

Au Vieux Bruxelles €–€€ *rue St-Boniface 35, tel: 02-503 3111,* www. auvieuxbruxelles.com. Situated close to the Porte Namur, this traditional restaurant is a proud purveyor of that Belgian seafood obsession, *moules*, served in a multiplicity of styles. It's been in business since 1882 and its mussels show no sign of flagging. Open Tue–Thu 6.30–11.30pm, Fri–Sat 6.30pm–midnight, Sun 6.30–11.30pm.

Blue Elephant €€ *chaussée de Waterloo 1120, tel: 02-374 4962.* On a long boulevard just west of the Bois de la Cambre, this top-rated Thai restaurant is celebrated for its delicate cuisine and enchanting setting. Open lunch Sun–Fri noon–2.30pm, dinner Mon–Fri 7–10.30pm, Sat–Sun until 11.30pm.

Brasseries Georges €–€€ *avenue Winston Churchill 259, tel: 02-347 2100,* www.brasseriesgeorges.be. Oysters are a signature item among multifarious seafood and meat dishes at this bustling brasserie, with a grand pavement terrace, on the corner of chaussée de Waterloo, just west of the Bois de la Cambre. Open Sun–Wed noon–11pm, Thu–Sat noon until midnight.

La Porte des Indes €€ *avenue Louise 455, tel: 02-647 8651,* www.laporte desindes.com/brussels. Facing the Abbaye de la Cambre, near the southern end of avenue Louise, this Indian restaurant is a delight to the senses and treats the cuisine of the subcontinent with the respect it deserves. Open daily dinner 7–10.30pm.

La Quincaillerie €€–€€€ *rue du Page 45, tel 02-533 9833,* www.quincaillerie.be. Situated near the Musée Horta, this brasserie-restaurant is housed in a late-19th-century warehouse. The industrial feel has been kept in the splendid décor, and the whole place hums with chatter. Belgian and continental dishes are on the menu here. Open lunch Mon–Sat noon–2.30pm, dinner daily 7pm–midnight.

ANTWERP

Grand Café De Rooden Hoed € *Oude Koornmarkt 25, tel: 03-289 0909*, www.deroodenhoed.be. Reputed to be Antwerp's oldest restaurant, this establishment, situated near the cathedral, opened in 1750. It provides hearty quantities of regional Belgian and French dishes, some of them old standbys and some modern. Open Tue–Fri noon–2pm, 6–9.30pm, Sat–Sun noon–2pm, 6–10pm.

Sir Anthony Van Dijck €€–€€€ *Oude Koornmarkt 16, tel: 03-231 6170*, www.siranthonyvandijck.be. Occupying a superb location in the restored 16th-century Vlaeykensgang courtyard, this modern French-Flemish restaurant is a labour of love for its owner-cum-chef, who removed himself from Michelin-star stress to do something that was considerably more to his liking. Open Tue–Sat noon–1.30pm and from 6.30pm.

BRUGES

Breydel-De Coninck €-€€ *Breidelstraat 24, tel: 050-339746*, http://restaurant-breydel.be. Situated in the street that connects the Burg and the Markt, this long-standing exponent of the Belgian obsession with mussels has traditional style and wood-beamed ceilings. It serves the multifaceted mollusc in a variety of ways. Other seafood dishes, such as lobster and eels, are on the menu too. Open Thu–Tue noon–2.30pm and 6.30–10pm.

Belgian Pigeon House €-€€ *Sint-Jansplein 12, tel: 050-661690*, www.belgianpigeonhouse.com. A grill restaurant in a medieval cellar where pigeons are the house speciality. The birds are bred especially for consumption but there are other meat and fish dishes to choose from – all oven-cooked over hot coals. Open Thu–Mon 11am–10pm.

Maximiliaan van Oostenrijk €-€€ *Wijngaardeplein 16–17, tel: 050-334723*, www.maximiliaanvanoostenrijk.be. A Burgundian restaurant in one of the city's most romantic areas, adjacent to the Begijnhof and the Minnewater (Lake of Love). Menu items include the traditional local stew *waterzooï*, along with grilled meats and seafood. Open daily 11am–11pm (closed Wed mid-Mar–mid-Nov).

Spinola €€ *Spinolarei 1, tel: 050-341785*, www.spinola.be. Traditional Flemish tapestries adorn the dining room of this, one of the best restaurants in town, just off Jan van Eyckplein. Fish dishes are a speciality. Open Tue–Sat, lunch noon–2pm, dinner 7–10pm.

GHENT

Belga Queen €–€€ *Graslei 10, tel: 09-280 0100*, www.belgaqueen.be. This beautiful gabled guild house features both a bar (on the second floor) and a restaurant (third floor). Tables by the window have wonderful views over the city's central canal. Serves traditional Flemish cuisine. Open daily, lunch noon–2.30pm, dinner 6.30–10.30pm, Fri–Sat until 11.30pm.

Keizershof € *Vrijdagmarkt 47, tel: 09-223 4446*, www.keizershof.net. Diners pile into hearty portions of Belgian and continental food in this large, rambling restaurant on Ghent's lively market square, amid a décor of wooden ceiling beams, plain wood tables and fashionably tattered walls. In summer, there's outdoor eating in the courtyard. Open Tue–Sat noon–2pm and 6–10pm.

A–Z TRAVEL TIPS

A SUMMARY OF PRACTICAL INFORMATION

A

ACCOMMODATION (see also Youth hostels and Budgeting for your trip)

Hotels are rated from one to five stars, based on their facilities, a rating indicated on a blue badge on the hotel's front door. The number of stars is not always a reliable guide to a hotel's quality. Some four-star hotels may have certain facilities yet still be unpleasant, while hotels further down the scale don't offer those facilities yet can be delightful. At the bottom end of the scale, below one star, are two letter-ratings: H for plain hotels and O for hotels that meet only the minimum legal standards. Serviced apartments and bed and breakfast accommodations are also available.

The high season is generally May to September, plus the Easter, Christmas and New Year holidays. Brussels has many business-oriented hotels that are generally busiest on weekdays from autumn to spring. Outside of the high season and at times when business and convention travel is slow, hotels are likely to offer steep discounts. Bruges, a popular tourist destination, is particularly busy in the summer months and at weekends.

The Brussels tourist office can make same-day reservations for you if you arrive without a booking. There is also a central reservations service for hotels in Belgium, Flex Appart; tel: 0-495 240 276; www.flexappart.be) or Custom Services (www.customservices.be).

Do you have a single/ double room? **Avez-vous une chambre pour une/deux personnes?** *Hebt u een eenpersoonskamer/tweepersoonskamer?*
with bath/shower? **avec bain/douche** *met een bad/douche*
What's the rate per night? **Quel est le prix pour une nuit?** *Hoeveel kost het per nacht?*

AIRPORT *(aéroport/luchthaven)*

Brussels Airport (BRU; tel: 0900-70000 in Belgium, +32-2-753 7753 from outside the country; www.brusselsairport.be) is the major international airport for all of Belgium. It lies 14km (9 miles) northeast of the city. There are frequent scheduled flights from other European cities, and many cities in the US and around the world.

Trains link the airport with the city centre 5.30am–12.30am (www.belgianrail.be). Departures are up to every 15 minutes. The journey time to Brussels-Nord is 15–20 minutes, and the fare is €9. These trains stop at the city's Gare du Nord, Gare Centrale and Gare du Midi stations, so it's helpful to know which station is nearest to your hotel. STIB Airport Line buses 12 and 21 run to the European District in Brussels. Bus 12 departs Mon–Fri until 8pm, while the service on route 21 operates Mon–Fri after 8pm and Sat–Sun; tickets cost €4.50, or €6 if bought on the bus (www.stib-mivb.be). De Lijn buses 272 and 471 depart hourly to Gare du Nord rail station; tickets cost €2 (or €3 if bought on the bus). Official taxis are black with yellow stickers. A taxi ride to the city centre takes about 25 minutes and costs about €45. Some taxis offer reduced-price return fares – look for a sticker in the corner of the windshield with a white aeroplane on an orange background.

Low-cost airlines, such as Ryanair and WizzAir, fly to **Brussels South Charleloi Airport** (CRL; tel: 0902-02490 in Belgium, +32-78-152722

Where can I get a taxi? **Où puis-je trouver un taxi?** *Waar kan ik een taxi nemen?*
How much is it to Brussels city centre? **Combien coûte la course jusqu'au centre de Bruxelles?** *Hoeveel kost het naar het centrum van Brussel?*
Does this bus go to Brussels? **Ce bus va-t-il à Bruxelles?** *Gaat deze bus naar Brussel?*

from outside the country; www.brussels-charleroi-airport.com), based in Charleloi, 60km (37 miles) south of the city.

There's a shuttle bus service between the Charleloi airport and the main Brussels railway station (Gare du Midi). The bus ride takes one hour, and vehicles leave every 30 minutes. You can buy your ticket at the terminal, onboard (when travelling from Brussels) or on-line (www. brussels-city-shuttle.com), which is the least expensive option. There are also nine shuttle buses per day leaving for Ghent and Bruges (www. flibco.com). Taxis are available outside the passenger terminal.

B

BICYCLE HIRE *(location de bicyclette/fietsverhuur)*
Getting around Brussels by bike is not recommended for anyone other than experienced, fit, nimble and stout-hearted cyclists. The city itself has a number of deceptive gradients and busy, aggressive traffic. Pro Velo offers bicycle hire and guided cycling tours of the city (rue de Londres 15; tel: 02-502 7355; www.provelo.org). A less arduous option is an electric bike tour (tel: 02-850 6090; http://onceinbrussels.be).

BUDGETING FOR YOUR TRIP
Here are a few sample prices to help with your budgeting.
Getting to Belgium. Many carriers, such as BA, BMI, Virgin Express and Aer Lingus, fly to Belgium from the UK and Ireland, and fares vary widely. Ryanair one-way fares to Brussels-Charleroi average £20–40 (€15–45) and can easily go higher.

Of the other options, going by bus from London is likely to be the cheapest. By train, Eurostar from London to Brussels offers good excursion and advance-purchase deals, as does the Channel Tunnel car-transporter. The cost of going by ferry to Zeebrugge or Ostend varies depending on the route, whether travelling as a foot passenger or with a car, and whether a cabin is desired. For a foot passenger, the price for a Hull–Zeebrugge return journey is approximately £230.

Accommodation. For a double room with bathroom and breakfast, you can pay less than €50, but for reasonable comfort and facilities, €75–100 is a more realistic starting point; a mid-range hotel will cost €100–250; and expensive hotels €250–500.

Eating out. You can eat well in many restaurants for less than €30 per person for a three-course meal without wine, but, a more reasonable starting point would be €40–50; in mid-range establishments, expect to pay €50–75; and in expensive restaurants, above €80.

Museums. Public museums charge €6–10 for adult admission. Privately owned attractions may cost about €20. Often, there are reduced rates for children, senior citizens and students. The Brussels Card offers free entry to 39 museums (24 hours €26; 48 hours €34; 72 hours €42; www. visit.brussels/en) and also reduced entry prices to many attractions and for an additional fee a public transport pass (see Tourist Information).

Public transport. Tickets for one journey (interchangeable between buses, trams and metro) cost €2.50 (€2.10 when purchased on board, €2 with a MOBIB card). If you have a Brussels Card and a STIB ticket, you can use all STIB buses, trams or metro lines around the Brussels region for 24, 48 or 72 hours. (see page 131).

C

CAR HIRE (location de voitures/autoverhuur)

With a city centre as compact as that in Brussels, and a well-organised public transport system, there is little need for a car. If you wish to explore the countryside, hiring a vehicle for a couple of days frees you from public transport schedules. All the major car-hire firms are represented in the city.

Your national driver's licence will be accepted, provided you have held it for at least a year. Minimum age limits for hiring vary between 20 and 25 years depending on the company and the size of your hire vehicle. Collision Damage Waiver is available, but expensive. Expect to pay about €100 per day for a small car.

Most major international firms have desks at Brussels Airport Arrivals Lounge, and offices around the city, and can be contacted for reservations as follows:

Avis: tel: 02-722 5831; www.avis.be.
Budget: tel: 02-720 0944; www.budget.be.
Hertz: tel: 02-720 6044 3201; www.hertz.be.
Europcar: tel: 02-721 0592; www.europcar.be.

CLIMATE

Brussels and the west of Belgium generally have warm, wet summers and cool, wet winters. In summer, there may be as many as seven hours of sunshine per day, with temperatures above 27°C (80°F); however, showers are always a possibility. Winter temperatures drop, but rarely fall below freezing. Rain can be expected just about every day. Average daytime temperatures in Brussels:

	J	F	M	A	M	J	J	A	S	O	N	D
°C	5	6	10	13	19	21	23	22	20	14	8	6
°F	41	43	50	55	66	70	74	72	68	57	46	41

CLOTHING

In summer, the weather can be pleasantly hot, and trousers, T-shirts, shirts and shorts will certainly be useful. However, do not forget to pack a warmer layer, in case there is a cold spell, and a rainproof outer layer. On most evenings you will require a jacket to walk around. In winter, pack warm clothing in addition to a waterproof layer. Don't forget comfortable shoes for sightseeing.

CRIME AND SAFETY (see also Emergencies and Police)

Belgium's current overall National Terrorism Threat Level indicates that a threat of terrorist attack still exists. In June 2017, there was a failed terrorist attack at Brussels central train station. In March 2016, terrorist attacks at Brussels National Airport (Zaventem) and at Maalbeek metro station in central Brussels killed 32 people and injured more than 300. Exercise particular caution around locations known to be possible terrorist targets. Monitor the news and other sources for changes to local conditions

Serious crime also exists and is a growing problem in some cities, including Brussels and Antwerp. Violent offences are rare, but drugs-related muggings and other crimes are increasing. After dark, stay alert if you are in metro and railway stations, or red-light areas; avoid deserted and poorly lit areas and stay out of city centre parks.

To minimise the risk of becoming a victim, take a few precautions. Do not carry large amounts of cash or valuables with you. Leave your valuables in the hotel safe. Carry all cash and credit cards in secure pockets. Keep handbags shut and carry them close to your body. Do not leave anything in your hire car, if you have one – crime involving vehicles is one of the most common crimes in the city. When walking back to your hotel at night, choose well-lit streets to reach your destination. It's also advisable to park your car in an area that is well lit.

D

DRIVING (see also Car hire)

To take your car into Belgium, you'll need:

an international driver's licence or your own driver's licence (held for at least one year),

car-registration papers,

Green Card (this does not provide cover, but is internationally recognised proof that you have insurance; though not obligatory for EU countries, it's still useful, especially in case of an accident),

a fire extinguisher and a red warning triangle and reflective jacket in case of breakdown,

a national identity sticker for your car,

> Are we on the right road for...? **Est-ce la bonne route pour...?** *Zijn wij op de juiste weg naar...?*

for right-hand-drive vehicles, headlight adapters to prevent the lights dazzling other drivers.

Driving conditions. Drive on the right, and pass on the left. Although you may wish to drive between towns and cities, it is ill-advised to drive within the big cities themselves. Driving is invariably aggressive, and there are complex one-way systems and intersections to negotiate, along with (in some cities) trams, which you are not allowed to overtake and to which you must give way.

Seat belts must be worn by both driver and passengers. The use of dipped headlights is mandatory after dusk and in poor visibility. There are stiff penalties for driving under the influence of alcohol and drugs, and for speeding. Some offences require payment of fines on the spot, with the offender's car impounded until payment is received.

Drivers should normally give way to traffic approaching from the right. A yellow diamond-shaped sign with a white border indicates that drivers on main roads have right of way; if the sign has a diagonal line through it, drivers give way to traffic entering from the right.

Motorways. Belgium's motorway *(autoroute/snelweg)* network is excellent, but it and the city ring roads, especially those of Brussels and Antwerp, can get congested at peak times. Other main roads are relatively free of traffic and weekday travelling is usually smooth. Belgium's accident record, however, is one of the worst in Europe.

Speed limits. On motorways, the limit is 120km/h (74mph); on other main roads it is 90km/h (55mph). In residential areas the speed limit is 50km/h (31mph). In all cases, lower limits may be indicated.

Parking. There is limited street parking in city centres. Car and coach parks exist in the centres, or in the case of pedestrian-friendly towns such as Bruges, around the perimeter of the centre.

Breakdowns. Belgium's two main motoring organisations are the Touring Club de Belgique and the Royal Automobile Club de Belgique. These have reciprocal arrangements with other national motoring organisations and should be able to help you if you are a member of your own national organisation. In case of breakdown, call Touring Secours/Wegenhulp, (tel: 070-344777; www.touring.be).

Fuel and oil: petrol stations are plentiful.

There's been an accident. **Il y a eu un accident.** *Er is een ongeval gebeurd.*

My car has broken down. **Ma voiture est en panne.** *Mijn wagen is kapot.*

E

ELECTRICITY

Belgium operates on 230 (220–240 volts), 50Hz AC, requiring standard two-pin round continental plugs.

EMBASSIES, CONSULATES AND HIGH COMMISSIONS

(ambassades; consulats/ambassades; consulaten)

Australia: avenue des Arts 56, Brussels, tel: 02-286 0500, www.belgium.embassy.gov.au.

Ireland: chaussée d'Etterbeek 180, Brussels, tel: 02-282 3400, www.dfa.ie/irish-embassy/belgium.

New Zealand: avenue des Nerviens 9–31, Brussels, tel: 02-512 1040, https://www.mfat.govt.nz/en/countries-and-regions/europe/belgium.

South Africa: rue Montoyer 17–19, Brussels, tel: 02-285 4400, www.southafrica.be.

UK: avenue d'Auderghem 10, Brussels, tel: 02-287 6211, www.gov.uk/government/world/belgium.

EMERGENCIES (see also Crime and safety and Police)

Police **101**

Ambulance **100**

Fire **100**

General emergency telephone number **112**

G

GAY AND LESBIAN TRAVELLERS

The vibrant gay and lesbian scene in Brussels is centred mainly in the Lower Town around rue du Marché-au-Charbon and rue des Riches-Claires. For information on Brussels and Wallonia, contact **Tels Quels** (rue Haute 48, Brussels; tel: 02-512 4587; www.telsquels.be), and La Maison Arc-en-Ciel (rue du Marché-au-Charbon 42, Brussels; tel: 02-503 5990; www.rainbowhouse.be). In Flanders, contact **Holebifoon** (tel: 09-223 6929; www.holebifoon.be). The age of consent for gay men is 16.

GETTING THERE

By air. Many airlines offer direct scheduled flights to Brussels Airport (see page 116). Brussels Airlines (tel: 0902 51600 in Belgium; www.brusselsairlines.com) is the main local carrier. British Airways (tel: 0844-493 0787 in the UK, 02-717 3217 in Belgium; www.britishairways.com) operates flights from several UK airports to Brussels. Flight time from London to Brussels is about one hour. Several other airlines operate flights from UK airports to Brussels. They include BMI (tel: 0330 333 7998 in the UK; in Belgium, tel: 02-588 0624; www.flybmi.com) and KLM (tel: 44 20 7660 0293 in the UK; in Belgium, tel: 02- 620 0220; www.klm.com). Aer Lingus (tel: 1880 800600 in Ireland; in Belgium, tel: 070-359901; www.aerlingus.com) has regular service to Brussels from Dublin and other Irish airports. Ryanair (tel: 0871-246 0000 in the UK; 1520 444 004 in Ireland, 0902-33600 in Belgium; www.ryanair.com) flies from Britain and Ireland to Charleroi, near Brussels.

By rail. A high-speed rail network, run by Belgian, Dutch, German and

French companies, operates between various cities in these countries. For reservations in Belgium, tel: 070-66 77 88; www.thalys.com.

Eurostar operates train services from London to Brussels. There are frequent departures and the journey time is just under two hours. You must make a reservation. For UK Eurostar reservations, tel: 03448 224 777, in Brussels, tel: 02-400 6731; www.eurostar.com.

Belgian state railways (SNCB/NMBS) operates local services within Belgium along with international services (tel: 02-528 2828; www.belgianrail.be).

By bus. National Express operates bus services between all the major European cities and Brussels (tel: 0871-78181 in the UK for bookings; www.nationalexpress.com).

By boat. Car ferries sail daily to Zeebrugge in Belgium from Hull in the UK (P&O Ferries; tel: 44 1304 448888 in the UK, 02-808 5020 in Belgium; www.poferries.com).

GUIDES AND TOURS *(guide/gids)*

Brussels offers a plethora of walking tours to suit all interests. Guided walks in English for individuals and groups are organised by Arkadia (rue Namur 10; tel: 02-319 4560; www.arkadia.be), Brukselbinnenstebuiten (Hopstraat 47; tel: 02-218 3878; www.brukselbinnenstebuiten.be), and Bravo Discovery (rue du Couloir 5; tel: 470 60 35 05; www.bravodiscovery.com), who also chocolate- and beer-tasting tours. For city tours covering art, architecture and culture, try ARAU (boulevard Adolphe Max 55; tel: 02-219 3345; www.arau.org). Music-lovers can follow in the footsteps of Jacques Brel with the aid of an audio-guide available for hire from Editions Jacques Brel (www.jacquesbrel.be). Those who wish to combine exercise and sightseeing should enjoy Brussels Sightjogging (http://brusselssightjogging.com). But if you feel like taking a rest, Brussels by Water is a more relaxing option (bis quai des Péniches 2; tel: 02-203 6406; www.brusselsbywater.be).

Brussels City Tours (rue du Marché aux Herbes 82; tel: 02-513 7744; www.brussels-city-tours.com), Le Bus Bavard (rue des Thuyas 12; tel: 02-673 1835; www.busbavard.be) and CitySightseeing Brussels (www.citysightseeingbrussel.be) operate bus tours around the city.

Calèche or horse-drawn carriage tours of the city centre are most popular in summer. They usually cover the Grand-Place and its surroundings. A 30-minute ride with a coachman-cum-guide costs approximately €44 per carriage. Horse carriages can be found throughout the year at rue Charles Buls (Grand-Place).

H

HEALTH AND MEDICAL CARE

Belgium has a sophisticated health-care system, and many doctors speak English. Medical care is expensive, so ensure that you are insured against illness or accident. For minor treatments, you may have to pay first and reclaim the payment from your insurance company later. Citizens from other European countries can obtain free medical treatment if they carry a European Health Insurance Card (EHIC).

Most prescription drugs are available in Belgium along with a large range of over-the-counter medications. A pharmacy *(pharmacie/apotheek)*, indicated by a green cross, will employ a qualified member of staff who will be able to advise you about treatments for minor ailments.

The **Cliniques Universitaires St-Luc** (avenue Hippocrate 10; tel: 02-764 1111; www.saintluc.be) has a casualty/emergency department.

Where's the nearest pharmacy? **Où est la pharmacie la plus proche?** *Waar is de dichtstbijzijnde apotheek?*
I need a doctor/dentist/ a hospital. **J'ai besoin d'un médecin/un dentiste/d'aller à l'hôpital.** *Ik heb een arts/tandarts/ziekenhuis nodig.*

L

LANGUAGE

About 60 percent of Belgians (mostly in the north of the country) speak Dutch (or *Nederlands*, as the language of Flanders and the Netherlands, is called). In Belgium, you will also hear it described as *Vlaams* – Flemish). In Wallonia (southern Belgium), most of the population speaks French. A small percentage of the population of the eastern part of the country speaks German.

Brussels itself is officially bilingual, with most people speaking French. You will find that many people in tourist situations speak English. The latter is, in fact, widely spoken, with many English-speaking expats living here. But do try using some French or Dutch, it really will be appreciated. *The Berlitz Phrase Book and Dictionary for French* and *The Berlitz Phrase Book and Dictionary for Dutch* cover most situations you are likely to encounter.

M

MEDIA

Newspapers and magazines. English-language newspapers and magazines are widely available. Expensive hotels often have free copies of the *International Herald Tribune, Financial Times* and other international newspapers. An English-language weekly news and events magazine, *The Bulletin*, is available in Brussels and other large towns (www.thebulletin.be).

Radio and television. The BBC World Service and European-based American networks can be picked up easily. Many hotels have cable television with up to 30 channels.

MONEY

The unit of currency in Belgium is the euro (€), divided into 100 cents. Coins are €2, €1 and 50, 20, 10, 5, 2 and 1 cents. Banknotes are €500,

€200, €100, €50, €20, €10 and €5 (the €500 and €200 notes are rarely if ever seen in normal circulation, and some small businesses may even be reluctant to accept €100 notes).

Exchange facilities. Generally, banks offer the best rates, followed by bureaux de change. Bureaux de change can be found at the airport, at each of Brussels' main railway stations and on and around the Grand-Place. Travellers' cheques can be cashed at these locations as long as you have your passport with you. There are currency-exchange machines at Brussels Airport which make transactions in several currencies. Cash machines (ATMs) called 'Bancontact' and 'Mister Cash', which accept non-Belgian cards, are widely available; the two Belgian brand names have been phased out in favour of the Maestro brand, but this makes no difference in practice.

Credit cards. Many hotels, restaurants and shops accept payment by international credit cards.

Can I pay by credit card? **Puis-je payer par carte bancaire?** *Mag ik met mijn kredietkaart betalen?*

I want to change some pounds/dollars **Je voudrais changer des livres sterling/dollars.** *Ik wil graag een paar pond/dollar wisselen.*

Can you cash a travellers cheque? **Changez-vous les cheques de voyage?** *Kan ik geld voor mijn reis cheque krijgen?*

Where's the nearest bank/currency exchange office? **Où est la banque/le bureau de change la/le plus proche?** *Waar is de dichtstbijzijnde bank/het dichtstbijzijnde wisselkantoor?*

Is there a cash machine here? **Y a-t-il un distributeur de billets?** *Is er hier ergens een geldautomaat?*

How much is that? **Combien coûte ceci?** *Hoeveel is dat?*

O

OPENING HOURS

Offices open from 8am or 9am until 5pm or 6pm Mon–Fri.

Shops are generally open from 10am to 6pm Mon–Sat, but tourist shops may stay open longer and open on Sun. Department stores are generally open until 8pm on Thu. Night-shops in the city, selling food, alcohol and other goods, are open until the early morning.

Banks are open Mon–Fri 9am–4 or 5pm, a few on Sat morning.

Museums are generally open Tue–Sat 10am–5 or 6pm, sometimes closing for one hour at lunchtime, usually between 1 and 2pm.

P

POLICE (see also Crime and safety and Emergencies)

The police (police/politie) can be reached on the emergency **101** telephone number. For less urgent police matters, go to **Brussels Central Police Station** (rue du Marché-au-Charbon 30, tel: 02-279 7711, near the Grand-Place).

POST OFFICES (La Poste/De Poste)

Belgian postal services are speedy and reliable. The main post office is at the Centre Monnaie in place de la Monnaie. Belgian post boxes are red with a stylised bugle in relief on the side. Postal rates for standard postcards and letters up to 50g in weight are €1.07 or €1.17 within Europe, and €1.29 or €1.39 for all other destinations. Post offices are usually open Mon–Fri, between 8.30 or 9am and 6pm. Bruxelles Bogards (rue des Bogards 19) and Bruxelles De Brouckère (boulevard Anspach 15) are the main post offices in the city centre.

PUBLIC HOLIDAYS

Belgium's national holiday (jour férié/openbare feestdag) days are:
1 January New Year's Day

1 May Labour Day
21 July National Day
15 August Assumption
1 November All Saints' Day
11 November Armistice Day (1918)
25 December Christmas
Movable dates: Easter Monday, Ascension Day, Pentecost Monday.

T

TELEPHONES

To call a number in Belgium from outside the country, first dial the international access code from the country you are in, followed by 32 (the country code for Belgium), and then the number minus the initial 0 of the area code. When making international calls from Belgium, dial 00 followed by the country code.

Roaming is possible on Belgium's tri-band and quad-band enabled GSM mobile-phone network. Phones to rent and to purchase, without a carrier subsidy (which is not permitted in Belgium), are widely available from phone stores, as are prepaid SIM cards for using your own (unlocked) phone at Belgian rates. Bring an appropriate plug adapter and, if needed, a voltage transformer for charging your phone.

TIME ZONES

Belgium is in the Central European Time zone, which is Greenwich Mean Time (GMT), or Universal Coordinated Time (UTC), plus one hour in winter and two hours in summer (between the end of March and the end of October, clocks are advanced one hour). Belgium is one hour

New York	London	**Belgium**	Jo'burg	Sydney	Auckland
6am	11am	**noon**	1pm	10pm	midnight

ahead of the UK and Ireland, six hours ahead of US Eastern Standard Time (but note that Daylight Saving Time begins at different times in the US), and 10 hours behind eastern Australia.

TIPPING

Service is included in most bills, so tipping is not necessary. Nevertheless, tips are still appreciated (though not always expected) by some service personnel, particularly in places that cater to a large number of tourists. To tip as Belgians do, in restaurants, round up your bill to the nearest convenient amount or leave about 5 percent. Service is also included in taxi fare rates.

TOILETS

In French-speaking areas of Belgium, toilets for females will generally be identified by the words Femmes or Mesdames, or their initial letter; toilets for men have Hommes or Messieurs. In Dutch-speaking areas, look for Damen and Heren. In Brussels, toilets may be indicated in both languages, or an appropriate image.

TOURIST INFORMATION

UK Belgian Tourist Office, Brussels & Wallonia, 217 Marsh Wall, London E14 9FJ, tel: 020-7537 1132, www.walloniabelgiumtourism.co.uk. Tourism Flanders-Brussels,1a Cavendish Square, London W1G 0LD, tel: 020-7307 7738, www.visitflanders.co.uk.

Brussels has its own **tourist information office (VisitBrussels)** at the Town Hall (Hôtel de Ville, Grand-Place; tel: 02-513 8940; http://visit.brussels.be). There are additional offices at rue Royale 2 and at Station Europe, Place du Luxembourg. There are also offices of the Wallonia and Flanders regional tourist organisations: Office de Promotion du Tourisme de Wallonie et de Bruxelles (rue St-Bernard 30, Brussels; www.opt.be) and Toerisme Vlaanderen (rue du Marché-aux-Herbes 61, Brussels; www.visitflanders.com).

Tourist offices in towns outside Brussels include:

Bruges Toerisme Brugge/In&Uit Brugge, Information Office Concertgebouw, 't Zand 34; Information office Markt, Markt 1; Information office Stationsplein, Stationsplein; tel: 050-444646; www.visitbruges.be.

Ghent Dienst Toerisme Gent/Infokantoor, Oude Vismijn, Sint-Veerleplein 5; tel: 09-266 5660; www.visitgent.be.

Antwerp Toerisme Antwerpen, Grote Markt 13 and Central Station, Koningin Astridplein; tel: 03-22 11333; www.antwerpen.be.

TRANSPORT

The Société de Transports Intercommunaux Bruxellois (STIB; tel: 070-232000, www.stib.be) runs metro, bus and tram services in the metropolitan area of Brussels. With one ticket you can transfer between trams, metro and buses for a period of one hour (you must re-validate your ticket with each change). STIB offices, metro stations and newsstands sell tickets. To buy a ticket from one of STIB's GO ticket machines, select "EVENT PASS" and follow the instructions on the screen. You must validate your ticket every time you use it. There is an electronic public transport pass called the MOBIB available at BOOTIK counters at principal metro stations. A single MOBIB fare is €5, while a single ticket is €2.10 (or €2.50 if purchased on board); a five-journey ticket costs €8, and a 10-journey ticket costs €14 (MOBIB). A 24-hour Discover Brussels pass costs €7.50, a 48-hour pass costs €14, and a 72-hour pass costs €18. These passes permit travel to and from the airport on lines 12 and 21 and are available from tourist offices, in addition to the other sources above. Public transport operates from 6am to midnight, and a limited night bus service covers the hours between midnight and 6am.

Metro. Metro (subway/underground) stations are indicated by a sign with a white M on a blue background.

Trams and buses. A network of trams and buses operates to all parts of the city. Red-and-white signs indicate stops for both. Signal the driver to stop if you want to get on.

Taxis. Fares start at €4,98, then €1.94 per km (0.6 mile) within greater Brussels. Contact: Taxi Bleus, (tel: 02-268 0000; www.taxisbleus.be); or Taxis Verts (tel: 02-349 4949; www.taxisverts.be).

Where can I get a taxi? **Où puis-je trouver un taxi?** *Waar kan ik een taxi nemen?*

What's the fare to...? **Quel est le prix de la course pour...?** *Hoeveel kost een rit naar...?*

When's the next bus/ train to...? **A quelle heure est le prochain bus/train pour...?** *Wanneer is de volgende bus/ trein naar...?*

I want a ticket to... **Je voudrais un billet pour...** *Ik wil graag een kaart naar...*

single/return **aller-simple/aller-retour** *enkele reis/retour* (also known as **un direct**/*een direkt*)

Trains. Belgian state railways (SNCB/NMBS; tel: 02-528 2828, www. belgianrail.be) operates services to Antwerp, Bruges and Ghent (and many other places). Excursion tickets include the cost of transport and the entrance fee for an attraction in certain areas.

Buses. For getting around outside the city, the bus is not as quick as the train, but for some destinations it is a more convenient option, and in some cases the only one. Walloon Brabant (mostly destinations south of Brussels) services are operated by TEC (tel: 010-235311; www.infotec. be); Flemish Brabant (mostly destinations north of Brussels) services are operated by De Lijn (tel: 070-220200; www.delijn.be).

V

VISAS AND ENTRY REQUIREMENTS

To enter Belgium for stays of up to three months, visitors from EU countries need only an identity card, or a passport if your country has no identity card. Citizens of most other countries, including Australia, New Zealand and South Africa, must be in possession of a valid passport, and in the case of some other countries, of a visa also. Residents of Europe and North America are not subject to health requirements; residents of other countries may be and should check with the local Belgian embassy or consulate before departure.

WEBSITES

www.walloniabelgiumtourism.co.uk Tourist office website covering Wallonia and French-speaking Brussels for the UK and Ireland.

www.visitflanders.co.uk Tourist office website covering Flanders and Flemish-speaking Brussels for the UK and Ireland.

www.visitbelgium.com Tourist office website for the US and Canada.

www.visitbrussels.be Website of the Brussels tourist office.

www.antwerpen.be Antwerp city website with a section on tourism.

www.brugge.be Bruges city website with a section on tourism.

www.visit.gent.be Ghent tourist office website.

www.resto.be Comprehensive restaurants information.

YOUTH HOSTELS *(auberge de jeunesse/jeugdherberg)*

The two national youth hostel associations are: Les Auberges de Jeunesse (rue de la Sablonnière 28, Brussels; tel: 02-219 5676; www.lesauberges-dejeunesse.be); and Vlaamse Jeugdherbergen (Beatrijslaan 72, Antwerp; tel: 03-232 7218; www.jeugdherbergen.be). Four good hostels are:

Auberge de Jeunesse Jacques Brel, rue de la Sablonnière 30, tel: 02-218 0187, www. lesaubergesdejeunesse.be. From €19.50 a night.

Génération Europe, rue de l'Eléphant 4, tel: 02-410 3858, www. lesaubergesdejeunesse.be. From €24 a night.

Jeugdherberg Breughel, rue du St-Esprit, tel: 02-511 0436, www.jeugdherbergen.be. From €21.70 a night.

Sleep Well, rue du Damier 23, tel: 02-218 5050, www.sleepwell.be. From €23 a night.

RECOMMENDED HOTELS

The prices below indicate room rates per night for a double room. Most budget and moderately priced hotels include breakfast in the room rate, but many expensive hotels do not. Older hotels tend not to have wheelchair access, although newer hotels generally have ramps. (For more information, see page 115.)

€€€€	over 400 euros
€€€	250–400 euros
€€	100–250 euros
€	below 100 euros

BRUSSELS

Grand-Place/Ilot Sacré/fish market

Amigo €€€ *rue de l'Amigo 1–3, tel: 02-547 4747,* www.roccofortehotels. com. One of the most luxurious hotels in the city, the Amigo is situated just off the Grand-Place.

Le Dixseptième €€€ *rue de la Madeleine 25, tel: 02-517 1717,* www.ledix-septieme.be. This intimate elegant hotel just across from the Galeries Royales St-Hubert was home to the Spanish ambassador in the 18th century, and the building retains much of its grandeur. All rooms have marble bathrooms.

Floris Arlequin Grand-Place €€ *rue de la Fourche 17–19, tel: 02-514 1615,* www.florishotelarlequin.be. Many rooms in this small hotel, situated in a historic district and street close to the Grand-Place and the Manneken-Pis, have beams and little windows. They are nicely furnished, but the bathrooms are small. You can't beat the location for both sightseeing and eating out.

George V € *rue T'Kint 23.* Modernised and generally brightened up, this small hotel in an old residential zone across the way from the Bourse, and a 10-minute walk from the Grand-Place, has quite basic but nicely furnished rooms.

Métropole €€€ *place de Brouckère 31, tel: 02-217 2300,* www.metropolehotel.be. The grande-dame of Brussels' hotels, the Métropole is sumptuous, with fantastic marble decorations, although some areas are showing their age. It has a fully equipped fitness centre.

Mozart €€ *rue du Marché-aux-Fromages 23, tel: 02-502 6661,* www.hotel-mozart.be. Situated one street behind the Grand-Place in the heart of a restaurant and bar area, the Mozart offers a good option to those who want to be very central. Rooms have antique furnishings and old paintings and the interiors are a flamboyant mix of Baroque and Oriental styles.

Residence le Quinze €€ *Grand-Place 15, tel: 02-511 0956,* www.hotel-le-quinze-grand-place.be. You can't get much closer to the Grand-Place than in the historic main square's only hotel. It has just 14 rooms, the more expensive with the most desirable view in town.

Welcome €€ *quai au Bois-à-Brûler 23, tel: 02-219 9546,* www.hotelwelcome.com. This boutique hotel, in a townhouse dating from 1896 at the Marché-aux-Poissons, makes up in personal attention for what it lacks in size. Each room is individually styled on a different national theme. There's no shortage of good seafood restaurants just outside on the Fish Market.

Upper City

Les Bluets € *rue Berckmans 124, tel: 02-534 3983,* www.bluets.be. In a townhouse dating from 1864 off avenue Louise, this small, quirky hotel, filled with antiques, is full of country-house charm, but just a 20-minute walk from the Grand-Place. The feeling of staying at a rural residence extends into the rooms, which are old-fashioned and comfortable rather than modern and efficient.

Eurostars Montgomery €€ *avenue de Tervueren 134, tel: 02-741 8511,* www.eurostarsmontgomery.com. Situated near Parc du Cinquantenaire, the Montgomery offers a variety of rooms, with decor ranging from blue marine with floral decorations to Japanese-style rooms in shades of blue and white. The library has volumes in several languages, and there's an elegant restaurant and a sauna.

9 Hotel Sablon €€ *rue de la Paille 2, tel: 02-880 0701,* www.9-hotel-sablon-brussels.be. A 4-star boutique hotel with attractive contemporary décor inspired by the artists and galleries of the Sablon district and luxurious spa facilities, including a swimming pool, hot tub and Finnish sauna. There's a bar but no restaurant, although there are plenty of dining options nearby.

Hotel du Congrès €€ *rue du Congrès 42, tel: 02-217 1890,* www.hoteldu congres.be. This hotel is just off rue Royale, about 15-minute walk from the Grand-Place. It's a clean, basic option, converted from four 19th-century houses. Some of the rooms overlook a garden.

Ibis Styles Brussels Louise €€ *avenue Louise 212, tel: 02-644 2929,* www. ibis.com. Stylish hotel in a pleasant district. The rooms in this converted townhouse are comfortable and rates are reasonable for a hotel on one of Brussels' most elegant streets.

Le Châtelain €€€€ *rue du Châtelain 17, tel: 02-646 0055,* www.le-chatelain.com. Luxury, five-star hotel, located just off avenue Louise. Rooms are lavishly equipped, tastefully furnished and well soundproofed. Guests can relax in an enchanting garden at the rear.

Made in Louise €€ *rue Veydt 40, tel: 02-537 4033,* www.madeinlouise. com. In a residential street off busy chaussée de Charleroi, this tranquil hotel is distinguished by graceful decor and antiques in its reception area and hallways. The rooms are plain, however, but mostly decently furnished, comfortable and cosy.

Pantone €€ *place Loix 1, tel: 02-541 4898,* www.pantonehotel.com. A palette of colours that ranges from fiery to restrained creates an up-to-the-minute ambiance in this designer hotel in a leafy part of the St-Gilles district, close to avenue Louise. Rooms also feature photography by Belgian artist Victor Levy. There's a rooftop bar terrace in summer.

Sabina €€ *rue du Nord 78, tel: 02-218 2637*, www.hotelsabina.eu. In a street off rue Royale, this small hotel in a 19th-century townhouse features some of the attributes of a private residence. The rooms don't quite match the warmth of the public spaces, but they are quiet and tastefully modern.

Steigenberger Wiltcher's €€€ *avenue Louise 71, tel: 02-542 4242*, http://en.steigenberger.com. Large and sprawling, this hotel on Brussels' grandest street is among the most expensive in town. Facilities include a heated indoor pool, a health club and spa, and a continental restaurant. The luxuriously furnished rooms include excellent amenities.

Vintage €€ *rue Dejoncker 45, tel: 02-533 9980*, www.vintagehotel.be. Housed in an early 20th-century townhouse close to avenue Louise, the retro-design vintage of this small hotel is broadly mid-20th century, and an in-house wine bar keeps the vintage theme going. Each bedroom has a unique decor.

Warwick Barsey €€€ *avenue Louise 381–383, tel: 02-649 9800*, www.warwickbarsey.com. A luxury hotel situated near the city centre and only minutes away from the best designer shopping in Brussels (on avenue Louise), the Warwick Barsey has well-furnished rooms, a bar and friendly helpful staff. Hotel guests can also enjoy a Renaissance-style terrace and garden.

Beyond the Old City

Bedford €€ *rue du Midi 135–137, tel: 02-507 0000*, www.hotelbedford.be. The Bedford is close to Gare du Midi. The decor in the rooms is a little unimaginative, and rooms also vary greatly in terms of natural light and noise levels. Restaurant, bar and shops.

Hotel Bloom! €€ *rue Royale 250, tel: 02-220 6611*, www.hotelbloom.com. New owners have reinvented the staid old Royal Crown, in the

Botanique district just outside the city centre, as an innovative, design-led hotel with a multifaceted continental restaurant. Not only does the hotel support artists and designers, but it also uses green electricity.

Le Plaza €€€€ *boulevard Adolphe Max 118–126, tel: 02-278 0100,* www.leplaza-brussels.be. Situated just a short stroll from place de Brouckère in an Art Deco palace, Le Plaza was a major attraction for visitors during the 1930s and 1940s, but it passed a number of years in the doldrums before being totally refurbished in fine style in the late 1990s.

Theater Hotel € *rue Van Gaver 23, tel: 02-350 9000,* www.theaterho telbrussels.com. This hotel is centrally located in the theatre district, close to Place Rogier and rue Nueve, and has a simple but cool contemporary style. Some rooms are triples and quads suitable for families or small groups.

Floris Ustel Midi €€ *square de l'Aviation 6–8, tel: 02-520 6053,* www. florishotelustelmidi.be. Friendly three-star hotel just minutes from Gare du Midi. There is a lively bar with a large terrace, and a fine restaurant, La Grande Ecluse (see page 111) is next door in the old flood-lock building of the River Senne. The hotel also features an entertainment room for guests.

ANTWERP

De Witte Lelie €€€ *Keizerstraat 16–18, tel: 03-226 1966,* www.dewit telelie.be. Magnificent suites-only hotel just minutes away from the Grote Markt and other attractions in central Antwerp. The courtyard is a peaceful retreat from the bustle of the city.

Rubenshof €€ *Amerikalei 115–117, tel: 03-237 0789,* www.rubenshof.be. Near the Royal Museum of Fine Arts, this small family hotel used to be the residence of Belgium's cardinal and features lavishly appointed public spaces. The 22 rooms are plain, but comfortable. The Art Nouveau breakfast room has beautiful stained-glass windows.

BRUGES

Die Swaene €€€ *Steenhouwersdijk 1, tel: 050-342798*, www.dieswaene. com. This small, romantic hotel on the Groenerei canal in the city centre has comfortable rooms elegantly and individually furnished to a high standard. Its lounge, from 1779, used to be the Guildhall of the Tailors. All rooms have separate bathrooms. The restaurant serves excellent seafood and Flemish cuisine.

Hans Memling €€ *Kuiperstraat 18, tel: 050-471212*, www.hansmemling. be. A small hotel situated in the heart of the city, the Hans Memling is perfect for exploring this historic town. It has a pleasant breakfast room and a cosy terrace.

Hotel Orangerie €€€ *Karthuizerinnenstraat 10, tel: 050-341649*, www. hotelorangerie.be. An attractive 17th-century canal house set opposite the Dijver canal, this hotel is in an ideal location. The rooms are individually designed and furnished to luxurious standards.

Rosenburg €€€ *Coupure 30, tel: 050-340194*, www.rosenburg.be. A 10-minute walk from the historic centre, this quiet, canal-side hotel offers plain modern yet comfortable accommodation. There is a restaurant and a bar. Most of rooms overlook the canal.

GHENT

NH Gent Belfort €€ *Hoogpoort 63, tel: 09-233 3331*, www.nh-hotels.com. Situated opposite the Stadhuis (Town Hall), the hotel is centrally located and in a perfect position for exploring the town. Facilities include a restaurant, bar, fitness room and sauna. Rooms are simple, yet stylish and spacious.

Novotel Gent Centrum €€ *Goudenleeuwplein 5, tel: 09-293 9002*, www. accorhotels.com. Part of the Accor chain, this is probably one of its most attractive hotels. Situated in the historic centre of Ghent, it incorporates a 14th-century crypt. There is a restaurant, a bar and an outdoor pool open in summer.

DICTIONARY

ENGLISH–FRENCH

adj adjective   **adv** adverb   **BE** British English   **n** noun   **prep** preposition   **v** verb

A

abbey l'abbaye
accept v accepter
access v accéder; n accès
accident l'accident
accommodation le logement
account le compte
acetaminophen le paracétamol
acupuncture l'acupuncture
adapter l'adaptateur
address l'adresse
admission l'entrée
after après; **~noon** l'après-midi; **~shave** l'après-rasage
age l'âge
agency l'agence
AIDS Déficience le Syndrome d'immuno-déficience acquise
air l'air; **~ con-ditioning** la climatisation; **~ pump** la pompe à air; **~line** la compagnie aérienne; **~mail** par avion; **~plane**

l'avion; **~port** l'aéroport
aisle (plane) le couloir; **~ (theater)** l'allée; **~ seat** le siège couloir
allergic allergique; **~ reaction** la -réaction al-lergique
allow v permettre
alone seul
alter v modifier
aluminum foil le papier aluminium
amazing surpre-nant
ambulance l'ambulance
American amé-ricain
amusement park le parc d'attractions
and et
anemic anémique
anesthesia l'anesthésie
animal l'animal
ankle la cheville
antibiotic l'antibiotique
antiques store l'antiquaire

antiseptic cream la crème antiseptique
anything rien
apartment l'appartement
appendix (body part) l'appendice
appetizer l'entrée
appointment le rendez-vous
arcade la salle de jeux
area code le code régional
arm le bras
aromatherapy l'aromathérapie
around (the cor-ner) au coin
arrivals (airport) les arrivées
arrive v arriver
artery l'artère
arthritis l'arthrite
art l'art
Asian asiatique
aspirin l'aspirine
asthmatic asthma-tique
ATM le distributeur automatique de billets; **~ card** la carte de retrait
attack l'attaque

attend v participer
attraction (place) le lieu touristique
attractive beau
Australia l'Australie
Australian australien
automatic automatique; **~ car** la voiture automatique
available dis-ponible

B

baby le bébé; **~ bottle** le biberon; **~ wipe** la lingette pour bébé; **~sitter** le baby-sitter
back (body part) le dos; **~ache** le mal de dos; **~pack** le sac à dos
bag le sac
baggage [BE] le bagage; **~ claim** le -retrait des bagages; **~ ticket** l'étiquette
bakery la boulangerie

ballet le ballet
bandage le pansement
bank la banque
bar (place) le bar
barbecue le barbecue
barber le coiffeur pour hommes
baseball le baseball
basket (grocery store) le panier
basketball le basketball
bathroom la salle de bains
battery la pile
battleground le champ de bataille
be v être
beach la plage
beautiful beau
bed le lit; **~ and breakfast** le bed and breakfast
before avant
begin v commencer
beginner le débutant
behind derrière
beige beige
belt la ceinture
berth la couchette
best meilleur
better mieux
bicycle la bicyclette; le vélo
big grand **~ bigger** plus grand
bike route la piste cyclable
bikini le bikini; **~ wax** l'épilation à la cire du maillot
bill (charge) v facturer; **~ n (invoice)** la facture; **~ n (money)** la coupure; **~ n (of sale)** le reçu
bird l'oiseau
birthday l'anniversaire
black noir
bladder la vessie
bland sans goût
blanket la couverture
bleed v saigner
blood le sang; **~ pressure** la tension
blouse le chemisier
blue bleu
board v embarquer; **~ing pass** la carte d'embarquement
boat le bateau
bone l'os
book le livre; **~store** la librairie
boots les bottes
boring ennuyant
botanical garden le jardin botanique
bother v ennuyer
bottle la bouteille; **~ opener** l'ouvre-bouteille
bowl le saladier
box la boîte
boxing match le match de boxe
boy le garçon;

~friend le petit-ami
bra le soutien-gorge
bracelet le bracelet
brakes (car) les freins
break v (tooth/bone) casser
breakdown la panne
breakfast le petit déjeuner
break-in (burglary) l'effraction
breast le sein; **~feed** v allaiter
breathe v respirer
bridge pont
briefs (clothing) les slips
bring v apporter
British anglais
broken cassé
brooch la broche
broom le balai
brother le frère
brown marron
bug l'insecte
building le bâtiment
burn v brûler
bus le bus; **~ station** la gare routière; **~ stop** l'arrêt de bus; **~ ticket** le ticket de bus; **~ tour** la visite en bus
business les affaires; **~ card** la carte de visite; **~ center** le

centre d'affaires; **~ class** la classe affaire; **~ hours** les heures d'ouverture
butcher le boucher
buttocks les fesses
buy v acheter
bye au revoir

C
cabaret le cabaret
cabin la cabine
cable car le téléphérique
café le café
call v appeler; **~ collect** appeler **~ n** l'appel en PCV;
calories les kilocalories
camera l'appareil photo; **~ case** le sac à appareil photo; **~ store** la boutique photo
camp v camper; **~ing stove** le réchaud; **~site** le camping
can opener le l'ouvre-boîte
Canada le Canada
Canadian canadien
cancel v annuler
candy le bonbon
canned goods les conserves
canyon la gorge

car la voiture;
~ hire [BE]
la voiture de
location; **~**
park [BE] le
parking; **rental**
~ la voiture de
location; **~ seat**
le siège bébé
carafe la carafe
card la carte; **ATM**
~ la carte de
retrait; **credit ~**
la carte de crédit;
phone ~ le carte
de téléphone
carry-on (piece of
hand luggage)
le bagage à main
cart le chariot
carton le paquet;
~ of
cigarettes la
cartouche de
cigarettes
case (amount)
le cas
cash v encaisser;
~ n le liquide;
~ advance
l'avance
cashier la caisse
casino le casino
castle le château
cathedral la
cathédrale
cave la grotte
CD le CD (disque
compact)
cell phone le
portable
Celsius Celsius
centimeter le
centimètre

certificate le
certificat
chair la chaise; **~**
lift le télésiège
change v **(baby)**
changer; **~ (mon-**
ey) échanger;
~ n **(money)** la
monnaie;
charcoal le
charbon de bois
charge v **(credit**
card) payer par
carte
charge (cost) le
coût
cheap bon marché
cheaper moins
cher
check v **(luggage)**
enregistrer; **~**
(on something)
vérifier; **~**
(payment) le
chèque; **~-in**
(hotel/airport)
l'enregistrement;
~ing
account le compte
courant; **~-out**
(hotel) quitter la
chambre
Cheers! Santé!
chemical toilet
les toilettes
portables
chemist [BE] la
pharmacie
cheque [BE] le
chèque
chest (body part)
la poitrine; **~ pain**
la douleur à la
poitrine

chewing gum le
chewing-gum
child l'enfant; **~'s**
seat le siège
enfant
children's menu le
menu enfant
children's portion
la portion enfant
chopsticks les
baguettes
church l'église
cigar le cigare
cigarette la
cigarette
class la classe
classical music
la musique
classique
clean v nettoyer;
~ adj propre; **~ing**
product le pro-
duit d'entretien;
~ing supplies
les produits
d'entretien
clear v **(on an ATM)**
effacer
cliff la falaise
cling film [BE] le
cellophane
close v **(shop)**
fermer; **~** adv
près; **~d** fermé
clothing les vête-
ments; **~ store**
le magasin de
vêtements
club le club
coat le manteau
coffee shop le café
coin la pièce
colander la
passoire

cold (sickness) le
rhume; **~ (tem-**
perature) froid
colleague le
collègue
cologne l'eau de
Cologne
color la couleur
comb le peigne
come v venir
complaint la
plainte
computer
l'ordinateur
concert le concert;
~ hall la salle de
concert
condition (medi-
cal) l'état de
santé
conditioner
l'après-sham-
pooing
condom le
préservatif
conference la
conférence
confirm v
confirmer
congestion la
congestion
connect v
(internet) se
connecter
connection
(flight) la
correspondance;
~ (internet) la
connexion
constipated
constipé
consulate le
consulat
consultant le

consultant
contact v contacter
contact lens les lentilles de contact; **~ solution** la solution pour lentilles de contact
contagious contagieux
convention hall le palais des congrès
conveyor belt le carrousel
cook v cuisiner; **~ing gas** le gaz
cool (temperature) frais
copper le cuivre
corkscrew le tire-bouchon
cost v coûter
cot le lit pliant
cotton le coton
cough v tousser; ~ n la toux
country code le code national
cover charge (bar, club) le droit d'entrée; **~ (restaurant)** le couvert
crash v **(car)** avoir un accident
cream (ointment) la crème
credit card la carte de crédit
crew neck le col rond
crib le berceau
crystal le cristal

cup la tasse
currency la monnaie; **~ exchange** l'échange de monnaie; **~ exchange office** le bureau de change
current account [BE] le compte courant
customs la douane
cut v couper; ~ n **(injury)** la coupure
cute mignon
cycling faire du vélo

D

damage v abîmer; **~d** endommagé
dance v danser; **~ club** la discothèque; **~ing** dansant
dangerous dangereux
dark sombre
date (calendar) la date
day le jour
deaf sourd
debit card la carte de retrait
deck chair la chaise longue
declare v déclarer
decline v **(credit card)** refuser
deeply profondément
degree (temperature) le degré

delay v retarder
delete v **(computer)** supprimer
delicatessen la charcuterie
delicious délicieux
denim jean
dentist le dentiste
denture le dentier
deodorant le déodorant
department store le grand magasin
departures (airport) les départs
deposit v déposer; **~ (bank)** le dépôt
desert le désert
detergent le détergent
develop v **(film)** développer
diabetic diabétique
dial v composer
diamond le diamant
diaper la couche
diarrhea la diarrhée
diesel le gazole
difficult difficile
digital numérique; **~ camera** l'appareil photo numérique; **~ photo** la photo numérique
dining room la salle à manger
dinner le dîner

direction la direction
dirty sale
disabled [BE] handicapé; **~ accessible [BE]** accessible aux handicapés
disconnect v **(computer)** déconnecter
discount la réduction
dish (kitchen) la vaisselle; **~washer** le lave-vaisselle; **~washing liquid** le détergent pour lave-vaisselle
display montrer; **~ case** la vitrine
disposable jetable; **~ razor** le rasoir jetable
dive v plonger; **~ing equipment** l'équipement de plongée
divorce v divorcer
dizzy avoir des vertiges
doctor le docteur
doll la poupée
dollar (U.S.) le dollar
domestic national; **~ flight** le vol national
door la porte
dormitory le dortoir
double bed le lit double

downtown (direction) vers le centre-ville; **~ area** le centre-ville
dozen la douzaine
drag lift le remonte-pentes
dress (piece of clothing) la robe; **~ code** la tenue exigée
drink *v* boire; **~** *n* la boisson; **~ menu** la carte des boissons
drinking water l'eau potable
drive *v* conduire; **~r's license number** le numéro de permis de conduire
drop (medicine) la goutte
drowsiness la somnolence
dry cleaner la teinturerie
dubbed doublé
during pendant
duty (tax) la taxe
duty-free hors taxe
DVD DVD

E

ear l'oreille; **~ache** l'otite
early tôt
earrings les boucles d'oreille
east est
easy facile

eat *v* manger
economy class la classe économique
elbow le coude
electric outlet la prise électrique
elevator l'ascenseur
e-mail *v* envoyer un mail; **~** *n* le mail; **~ address** l'adresse mail
emergency l'urgence; **~ exit** la sortie de secours
empty *v* vider
enamel (jewelry) l'émail
end *v* finir
English anglais
engrave *v* graver
enjoy *v* prendre plaisir
enter *v* entrer
entertainment le divertissement
entrance l'entrée
envelope l'enveloppe
equipment l'équipement
escalators l'escalator
e-ticket le billet électronique
EU resident le résident européen
euro l'euro
evening la soirée
excess l'excès
exchange *v* échanger; **~** *n;*

(place) le bureau de change; **~ rate** le taux de change
excursion l'excursion
excuse *v* excuser
exhausted épuisé
exit *v* sortir; **~** *n* la sortie
expensive cher
expert (skill level) l'expert
exposure (film) la pose
express express; **~ bus** le bus direct; **~ train** l'express
extension (phone) le poste
extra extra; **~ large** très grand
extract *v* **(tooth)** arracher
eye l'œil
eyebrow wax l'épilation à la cire des sourcils

F

face le visage
facial le soin du visage
family la famille
fan (appliance) le ventilateur; **~ (souvenir)** l'éventail
far loin
farm la ferme
far-sighted presbyte
fast vite; **~ food** le fast food

faster plus vite
fat free 0% de matières grasses
father le père
fax *v* envoyer un fax; **~** *n* le fax; **~ number** le numéro de fax
feed *v* nourrir
ferry le ferry
fever la fièvre
field (sports) le terrain de sport
fill *v* faire le plein
fill *v* **out (form)** remplir
filling (tooth) le plombage
film (camera) la pellicule
fine (fee for breaking law) la contravention
finger le doigt; **~nail** l'ongle
fire le feu; **~ department** les pompiers; **~ door** la porte coupe-feu
first premier; **~ class** la première classe
fitting room la cabine d'essayage
fix *v* **(repair)** réparer
flashlight la lampe torche
flat tire [tyre BE] le pneu crevé
flight le vol
floor le sol

flower la fleur
folk music la musique folklorique
food la nourriture
foot le pied
football [BE] le football; **~ game [BE]** le match de football
for pour
forecast la météo
forest la forêt
fork la fourchette
form le formulaire
formula (baby) le lait pour bébés
fort le fort
fountain la fontaine
France la France
free libre
freezer le congélateur
French français
fresh frais
friend l'ami
frying pan la poêle
full-service le service complet
full-time le temps plein

G

game le match
garage le garage
garbage bag le sac poubelle
gas l'essence; **~ station** la station service
gate (airport) la porte

gay gay; **~ bar** le bar gay; **~ club** le club gay
gel (hair) le gel
get off v (a train, bus, subway) descendre
get to v aller
gift le cadeau; **~ shop** la boutique cadeaux
girl la fille; **~friend** la petite-amie
give v donner
glass le verre;
glasses les lunettes
go v (somewhere) aller
gold l'or
golf course le terrain de golf
golf tournament le tournoi de golf
good adj bon; **~** n le produit; **~ afternoon** bon après-midi; **~ evening** bonsoir; **~ morning** bonjour; **~bye** au revoir
goods les produits
gram le gramme
grandchild les petits-enfants
grandparent les grands-parents
gray gris
green vert
grocery store le magasin de fruits et légumes
ground floor le rez-de-chaussée

groundcloth le tapis de sol
groundsheet le drap du dessous
group le groupe
guide le guide; **~ book** le guide; **~ dog** le chien d'aveugle
gym la gym
gynecologist le gynécologue

H

hair les cheveux; dryer le sèche-cheveux d'étudiant; **~ salon** le coiffeur; **~brush** la brosse; **~cut** la coupe de cheveux; **~spray** la laque; **~style** le style de coiffure; **~stylist** le coiffeur
half la moitié; **~ hour** la demi-heure **~kilo** le demi-kilo
hammer le marteau
hand la main; **~ luggage [BE]** le bagage à main; **~bag [BE]** le sac à main
handicapped l'handicapé; **~-accessible** accessible aux handicapés
hangover la gueule de bois

happy heureux
hat le chapeau
have v avoir
head (body part) la tête; **~ache** le mal de tête; **~phones** les écouteurs
health la santé; **~ food store** le magasin de produits diététiques
heart le cœur; **~ condition** le problème cardiaque
heat le chauffage; **~er** le chauffage
hectare l'hectare
hello bonjour
helmet le casque
help v aider; **~** n l'aide
here ici
hi salut
high haut; **~chair** la chaise haute; **~-heeled shoes** les chaussures à talons aiguilles; **~way** l'autoroute
hiking boots les chaussures de marche
hill la colline
hire v [BE] louer; **~ car [BE]** la voiture de location
hitchhike v faire de l'auto-stop
hockey le hockey
holiday [BE] les vacances

horsetrack le champ de course
hospital l'hôpital
hostel l'auberge de jeunesse
hot (spicy) épicé; **~ (temperature)** chaud; **~ spring** la source chaude; **~ water** l'eau chaude
hotel l'hôtel
hour l'heure
house la maison; **~hold goods** les produits ménagers; **~keeping service** le service d'entretien
how comment; **~ much** combien
hug v enlacer
hungry faim
hurt la douleur
husband le mari

I

ibuprofen l'ibuprofène
ice la glace; **~ hockey** le hockey sur glace
icy glacé
identification l'identification
ill malade
in dans
include v inclure
indoor pool la piscine intérieure
inexpensive pas cher
infected infecté

information (phone) les renseignements; **~ desk** le bureau des renseignements
insect l'insecte; **~ bite** la piqure d'insecte; **~ repellent** la lotion anti-insectes
insert v insérer
insomnia l'insomnie
instant message le message instantané
insulin l'insuline
insurance l'assurance; **~ card** la carte d'assurance; **~ company** la compagnie d'assurance
interesting intéressant
intermediate le niveau intermédiaire
international (airport area) l'international (terminal); **~ flight** le vol international; **~ student card** la carte internationale d'étudiant
internet l'internet; **~ cafe** le cyber café; **~ service** le service internet
interpreter l'interprète

intersection l'intersection
intestine l'intestin
introduce v présenter
invoice [BE] la facture
Ireland l'Irlande
Irish irlandais
iron v repasser; **~ n (clothes)** le fer à repasser
Italian italien

J

jacket la veste
jar le pot
jaw la mâchoire
jazz le jazz; **~ club** le club de jazz
jeans le jean
jet ski le jet ski
jeweler la bijouterie
jewelry le bijou
join v joindre
joint (body part) l'articulation

K

key la clé; **~ card** la carte de la chambre; **~ ring** la chaîne
kiddie pool la pataugeoire
kidney (body part) le rein
kilo le kilo; **~gram** le kilogramme; **~meter** le kilomètre
kiss v embrasser

kitchen la cuisine; **~ foil [BE]** le papier aluminium
knee le genou
knife le couteau

L

lace la dentelle
lactose intolerant allergique au lactose
lake le lac
large grand
larger plus grand
last dernier
late (time) tard
later plus tard
laundromat la laverie automatique
laundry la lessive; **~ facility** la buanderie; **~ service** le service de nettoyage
lawyer l'avocat
leather le cuir
leave v partir
left (direction) à gauche
leg la jambe
lens le verre
less moins
lesson la leçon
letter la lettre
library la bibliothèque
life jacket le gilet de sauvetage
lifeguard le secouriste
lift [BE] l'ascenseur; **~ pass** le forfait

light (cigarette) v allumer; ~ adj **(overhead)** blond; **~bulb** l'ampoule
lighter le briquet
like v aimer
line (train) la ligne
linen le lin
lip les lèvres
liquor store le marchand de vins et de spiritueux
liter le litre
little adv peu; ~ adj petit
live v vivre
liver (body part) le foie
loafers les mocassins
local du quartier
lock v fermer; ~ n le cadenas; **~er** la consigne
log off (computer) terminer une session
log on (computer) ouvrir une session
long long; ~ **sleeves** les manches longues; **~-sighted [BE]** presbyte
look v regarder
lose v (something) perdre
lost perdu; **~ and found** les objets trouvés
lotion la crème
louder plus fort

love v (someone) aimer; ~ n amour
low bas
luggage le bagage; **~ cart** le chariot; **~ locker** la consigne; **~ ticket** le retrait des bagages
lunch le déjeuner
lung le poumon

M

magazine le magazine
magnificent magnifique
mail le courrier; **~box** la boîte-à-lettres
main attraction la principale attraction touristique
main course le plat principal
mall le centre commercial
man l'homme
manager le responsable
manicure la manucure
manual car la voiture manuelle
map la carte
market le marché
married marié
marry v se marier
mass (church service) la messe
massage le massage
match le match

meal le repas
measure v (someone) mesurer
measuring cup la mesure
measuring spoon la cuillère à doser
mechanic le mécanicien
medicine le médicament
medium (size) moyen
meet v (someone) rencontrer
meeting la réunion; **~ room** la salle de réunion
membership card la carte de membre
memorial (place) le lieu commémoratif
memory card la carte mémoire
mend v raccourcir
menstrual cramp les règles douloureuses
menu la carte
message le message
meter (parking) l'horodateur
microwave le micro-onde
midday [BE] midi
midnight minuit
mileage le kilométrage
mini-bar le mini bar
minute la minute
missing disparu

mistake l'erreur
mobile home le mobile home
mobile phone [BE] le portable
mobility la mobilité
money l'argent
month le mois
mop la serpillière
moped la mobylette
more plus
morning le matin
mosque la mosquée
mother la mère
motion sickness (air) le mal de l'air; **~ (sea)** le mal de mer
motor boat le bateau à moteur
motorcycle la mobylette
motorway [BE] l'autoroute
mountain la montagne mousse la mousse
mouth la bouche
movie le film; **~ theater** le cinéma
mug v attaquer
muscle le muscle
museum le musée
music la musique; **~ store** le disquaire

N

nail file la lime á ongle

nail salon l'onglerie
name le nom
napkin la serviette
nappies [BE] les couches
nationality la nationalité
nature preserve la réserve naturelle
nausea la nausée
near près;
~**by** près de;
~-**sighted** myope
neck le cou
necklace le collier
need v avoir besoin
newspaper le journal
newsstand le kiosque à journaux
next suivant
nice bien
night la nuit
nightclub le night club
no non
non-alcoholic non alcoolisé
non-smoking non fumeur
noon midi
north nord
nose le nez
note [BE] la coupure
nothing rien
notify v informer
novice (skill level) novice
now maintenant
number le nombre; le numéro
nurse l'infirmier

O
office le bureau; ~ **hours** les heures d'ouverture
off-licence [BE] le marchand de vins et de spiritueux
oil l'huile
OK d'accord
old vieux
on the corner au coin
once une fois
one un; ~-**way (ticket)** l'aller simple; ~-**way street** le sens unique
only seulement
open v ouvrir; ~ adj ouvert
opera l'opéra; ~ **house** l'opéra
opposite le contraire
optician l'opticien
orange (color) orange
orchestra l'orchestre
order v commander
outdoor pool la piscine extérieure
outside dehors
over-the-counter (medication) sans ordonnance
overlook (scenic place) le point d'observation
overnight de nuit
oxygen treatment le soin à l'oxygène

P
pacifier la tétine
pack v faire les bagages
package le colis
pad [BE] la serviette hygiénique
pain la douleur
pajamas le pyjama
palace le palais
panties les culottes
pants le pantalon
pantyhose le collant
paper le papier; ~ **towel** la serviette en papier
paracetamol [BE] le paracétamol
park v se garer; ~ n le parc; ~**ing garage** le garage; ~**ing lot** le parking
part (for car) la pièce; ~-**time** le temps partiel
pass through v passer
passenger le passager
passport le passeport; ~ **control** le contrôle de passeport
password le mot de passe
pastry shop la pâtisserie
path le chemin
pay v payer; ~ **phone** le téléphone public

peak (of a mountain) le sommet
pearl la perle
pedestrian le piéton
pediatrician le pédiatre
pedicure la pédicure
pen le stylo
penicillin la pénicilline
penis le pénis
per par; ~ **day** par jour; ~ **hour** par heure; ~ **night** par nuit; ~ **week** par semaine
perfume le parfum
period (menstrual) les règles; ~ **(of time)** la période
permit v permettre
personal identification number (PIN) le code secret
petite menue
petrol [BE] le l'essence; ~ **station [BE]** la station service
pewter l'étain
pharmacy la pharmacie
phone v téléphoner; ~ n le téléphone; ~ **call** l'appel; ~ **card** la carte de téléphone; ~ **number** le numéro de téléphone

photo la photo; **~copy** la photocopie; **~graphy** la photographie

pick up v **(something)** prendre

picnic area l'aire de pique-nique

piece le morceau

Pill (birth control) la pilule

pillow l'oreiller

pink rose

piste [BE] la piste; **~ map [BE]** la carte des pistes

pizzeria la pizzeria

place v **(a bet)** parier

plane l'avion

plastic wrap le cellophane

plate l'assiette

platform le quai

platinum platine

play v jouer; **~** n (theater) la pièce **~ground** l'aire de jeux **~pen** le parc

please s'il vous plaît

pleasure le plaisir

plunger le déboucheur de toilettes

plus size grande taille

pocket la poche

poison le poison

poles (skiing) les bâtons

police la police; **~ report** le rapport de police; **~ station** le commissariat de police

pond l'étang

pool la piscine

pop music la pop musique

portion la portion

post [BE] le courrier; **~ office** le bureau de poste; **~box [BE]** la boîte-à-lettres; **~card** la carte postale

pot la casserole

pottery la poterie

pound (British sterling) la livre sterling

pregnant enceinte

prescribe v prescrire

prescription l'ordonnance

press v **(clothing)** repasser

price le prix

print v imprimer

problem le problème

produce v produire; **~ store** le marchand de fruits et légumes

prohibit v interdire

pronounce v prononcer

public public

pull v **(door sign)** tirer

purple pourpre

purse le sac

push v **(door sign)** pousser

pushchair [BE] la poussette

Q

quality la qualité

question la question

quiet le silence; le calme

R

racetrack la piste de courses

racket (sports) la raquette

railway station [BE] la gare

rain la pluie; **~coat** l'imperméable; **~forest** la forêt vierge

rainy pluvieux

rap (music) le rap

rape v violer; **~** n le viol

rash l'irritation cutanée

razor blade la lame de rasoir

reach v atteindre

ready prêt

real vrai

receipt le reçu

receive v recevoir

reception la réception

recharge v recharger

recommend v recommander

recommendation la recommanda-tion

recycling les ordures à recycler

red rouge

refrigerator le réfrigérateur

region la région

registered mail le courrier recom-mandé

regular ordinaire

relationship la relation

rent v louer; **~al car** la voiture de location

repair v réparer

repeat v répéter

reservation la réservation; **~ desk** le bureau de réservation

reserve v réserver

restaurant le restaurant

restroom les toilettes

retired v prendre sa retraite

return v **(something)** rendre; **~** n **[BE]** l'aller-retour

rib (body part) la côte

right (direction) à droite; **~ of way** le droit de passage

ring la bague

river la rivière

road map la carte routière

rob v voler

romantic romantique

room la pièce; **~ key** la clé; **~ service** le service de chambre

round-trip l'aller-retour

route la route

rowboat la barque

rubbish [BE] les poubelles; **~ bag [BE]** le sac poubelle

rugby le rugby

ruins les ruines

S

sad triste

safe adj en sécurité; **~ n** le coffre-fort

sales tax la TVA

same le même

sandals les sandales

sanitary napkin la serviette hygiénique

saucepan la casserole

sauna le sauna

save v (computer) sauvegarder

savings (account) le compte épargne

scanner scanner

scarf l'écharpe

schedule v prévoir; **~ n** l'horaire

science la science

scissors les ciseaux

sea la mer

seat le siège

security la sécurité

see v voir

self-service le self-service

sell v vendre

seminar le séminaire

send v envoyer

senior citizens les seniors

separated (marriage) séparés

serious sérieux

service (in a restaurant) le service

sexually transmitted disease (STD) les maladies sexuellement transmissibles

shampoo le shampooing

sharp tranchant

shaving cream la mousse à raser

sheet le drap

shirt la chemise

ship v envoyer

shoe store le magasin de chaussures

shoes les chaussures

shop v faire des achats

shopping les courses; **~ area** le quartier des magasins; **~ centre [BE]** le centre commercial; **~**

mall le centre commercial

short court; **~-sighted [BE]** myope; **~ sleeves** les manches courtes; **~s** le short

shoulder l'épaule

show v montrer

shower la douche

shrine le lieu saint

sick malade

side dish l'accompagnement

side effect l'effet secondaire

sightseeing le tourisme; **~ tour** la visite touristique

sign v signer

silk la soie

single (unmarried) adj célibataire; n **~ bed** le lit une place; **~ prints** le tirage unique; **~ room** la chambre simple

sink l'évier

sister la sœur

sit v s'asseoir

size la taille

ski v skier; **~ n** le ski; **~ lift** le télésiège

skin la peau

skirt la jupe

sleep v dormir

sleeper car le wagon couchette

sleeping bag le sac de couchage

sleeping car [BE] le wagon couchette

slice la tranche

slippers les chaussons

slower plus lent

slowly lentement

small petit

smaller plus petit

smoke v fumer

smoking (area) la zone fumeur

snack bar le bar

sneakers les tennis

snorkeling equipment l'équipement de plongée

snowboard le snowboard

snowshoe la chaussure de ski

snowy neigeux

soap le savon

soccer le football; **~ game** le match de football

sock la chaussette

soother [BE] la tétine

sore throat le mal de gorge

sorry désolé

south sud

souvenir le souvenir; **~ store** le magasin de souvenirs

spa le spa

spatula la spatule
speak v parler
special (food) la spécialité; le plat typique
specialist (doctor) le spécialiste
specimen l'échantillon
speed (velocity) la vitesse
spell v épeler
spicy épicé
spine (body part) la colonne vertébrale
spoon la cuillère
sporting goods store le magasin de sport
sports le sport; ~ massage le massage sportif
sprain l'entorse
stadium le stade
stairs les escaliers
stamp v (a ticket) timbrer; ~ n (postage) le timbre
start v (a car) démarrer; v (to begin) commencer
starter [BE] l'entrée
station la station; ~ wagon la break; bus ~ la gare routière; gas ~ la station service; muster

~ [BE] la salle d'attente; petrol ~ [BE] la station service; subway ~ la station de métro; train ~ la gare
statue la statue
stay v rester
steal v voler
steep escarpé
sterling silver l'argent fin
sting la piqûre
stolen volé
stomach l'estomac; ~ache les maux de ventre
stop v arrêter; ~ n l'arrêt
store directory le plan du magasin
stove la gazinière
straight droit
strange étrange
stream le ruisseau
stroller la poussette
student l'étudiant
study v étudier
stunning stupéfiant
subtitle subtil
subway le métro; ~ station la station de métro
suit le costume; ~case la valise
sun le soleil; ~ block l'écran solaire; ~burn le coup de soleil; ~glasses les lunettes de soleil
sunny ensoleillé

sunscreen la crème solaire
sunstroke l'insolation
super (fuel) le super; ~market le supermarché; ~vision la supervision
surfboard le surf
swallow v avaler
sweater le pull
sweatshirt le sweat-shirt
sweet (taste) sucré
sweets [BE] les bonbons
swell v gonfler
swim v nager
swimsuit le maillot de bain
symbol (keyboard) le symbole
synagogue la synagogue

T

table la table
tablet (medicine) le cachet
take v prendre
take away [BE] à emporter
tampon le tampon
taste v goûter
taxi le taxi
team l'équipe
teaspoon la cuillère à café
telephone le téléphone
temple (religious) le temple

temporary temporaire
tennis le tennis
tent la tente; ~ peg le piquet; ~ pole le pilier
terminal (airport) le terminal
terracotta la terre cuite
terrible terrible
text v (send a message) écrire; ~ n (message) le texte
thank v remercier; ~ you merci
that ça/cela
theater le théâtre
theft le vol
there là
thief le voleur
thigh la cuisse
thirsty soif
this ceci
throat la gorge
ticket le billet; ~ office la billetterie
tie (clothing) la cravate
time le temps; ~table [BE] les horaires
tire [tyre BE] le pneu
tired fatigué
tissues les Kleenex
to go aller
tobacconist le tabac
today aujourd'hui

toe l'orteil; **~nail** l'ongle
toilet [BE] les toilettes; **~ paper** le papier toilette
tomorrow demain
tongue la langue
tonight ce soir
too trop
tooth la dent; **~paste** le dentifrice
total (amount) le total
tough (food) dur
tour la visite
tourist le touriste; **~ information office** le syndicat d'initiative
tow truck la dépanneuse
towel la serviette
tower la tour
town la ville; **~ hall** la mairie; **~ map** la carte de la ville; **~ square** le centre ville
toy le jouet; **~ store** le magasin de jouets
track (train) le quai
traditional traditionnel
traffic light le feu tricolore
trail la piste; **~ map** la carte des pistes
trailer la remorque
train le train; **~ station** la gare

translate v traduire
trash les poubelles
travel v voyager; **~ agency** l'agence de voyage; **~ sickness** le mal des transports; **~er's check [cheque BE]** le chèque de voyages
tree l'arbre
trim (hair cut) v égaliser
trip le voyage
trolley [BE] le chariot
trousers [BE] le pantalon
T-shirt le t-shirt
turn off v **(lights)** éteindre
turn on v **(lights)** allumer
TV la télé
type v taper

U

ugly laid
umbrella le parapluie
unattended sans surveillance
unbranded medication [BE] le médicament générique
unconscious inconscient
underground [BE] le métro; **~ station [BE]** la station de métro
underpants [BE] les slips

understand v comprendre
underwear les sous-vêtements
United Kingdom (U.K.) le Royaume Uni
United States (U.S.) les États-Unis
university l'université
unleaded (gas) sans plomb
upper supérieur
urgent urgent
use v utiliser
username le nom de l'utilisateur
utensil l'ustensile

V

vacancy libre
vacation les vacances
vaccination la vaccination
vacuum cleaner l'aspirateur
vagina le vagin
vaginal infection l'infection vaginale
valid valide
valley la vallée
valuable précieux
value la valeur
VAT [BE] la TVA
vegetarian végétarien
vehicle registration la carte grise
viewpoint [BE] le point d'observation

village le village
vineyard le vignoble
visit v visiter; **~ing hours** les heures de visite
visually impaired le malvoyant
vitamin la vitamine
V-neck le col en V
volleyball game le match de volleyball
vomit v vomir

W

wait v attendre; **~** n l'attente
waiter le serveur
waiting room la salle d'attente
waitress la serveuse
wake v réveiller; **~-up call** n l'appel réveil
walk v marcher; **~** n la promenade; **~ing route** le chemin de randonnée
wall clock la pendule
wallet le portefeuille
warm (something) v réchauffer **~** adj **(temperature)** chaud
washing machine la machine à laver
watch la montre
water skis les skis nautiques

waterfall la cascade
weather le temps
week la semaine; **~week-end** le week-end
weekly hebdomadaire
welcome *v* accueillir
well-rested bien reposé
west ouest
what quoi
wheelchair la chaise roulante; **~ ramp** la rampe d'accès

when quand
where où
white blanc; **~ gold** l'or blanc
who qui
widow le veuf
wife l'épouse
window la fenêtre; **~ case** le chambranle
windsurfer le véliplanchiste
wine list la carte des vins

wireless internet l'accès Wi-Fi
wireless phone le portable
with avec
withdraw *v* retirer
withdrawal (bank) le retrait
without sans
woman la femme
wool la laine
work *v* travailler
wrap *v* emballer
wrist le poignet
write *v* écrire

Y

year l'année
yellow jaune; **~ gold** l'or jaune
yes oui
yesterday hier
you're welcome de rien
young jeune
youth hostel l'auberge de jeunesse

Z

zoo le zoo

ENGLISH-DUTCH

A

about
(approximately)
ongeveer;
(regarding) over
above boven
abroad in het
buitenland
accept accepteren
access toegang
accident ongeluk
accidentally per
ongeluk
accommodations
logies
accompany
meegaan
acetaminophen
paracetamol
acne acne
across naar de
overkant
acupuncture
acupunctuur
adapter adapter
additional extra
address adres
adjoining
aangrenzend
admission charge
toegangsprijs
adult volwassene
after na
afternoon middag
aftershave
aftershave
agree akkoord gaan
air lucht
air conditioning
airco

air mattress
luchtbed
air pump
luchtpomp
airmail luchtpost
airport vliegveld
airsickness
luchtziekte
aisle gangpad
alarm clock
wekker
all alle
allergic allergisch
allergy allergie
alley steegje
all-night pharmacy
nachtapotheek
allow toestaan
allowance
(quantity)
toegestane
hoeveelheid;
(permit)
vergunning
almost bijna
alone alleen
already al
also ook
alter vermaken
alternate adj
alternatief
aluminum foil
aluminiumfolie
always altijd
amazing
verbazingwekkend
ambassador
ambassadeur
ambulance
ambulance

American
n Amerikaan;
adj Amerikaans
amount (money)
bedrag;
(quantity)
hoeveelheid
amusement park
pretpark
anesthetic
verdovingsmiddel
and en
anemia
bloedarmoede
animal dier
another een ander
antacid antacidum
antibiotics
antibiotica
antifreeze
antivries
antique antiek
antiseptic
adj antiseptisch
any wat
anyone iemand
anything iets
apartment
appartement
apologize zich
verontschuldigen
appendix
blindedarm
appetite eetlust
appointment
afspraak
approve
goedkeuren
approximately
ongeveer

arcade speelhal
area code
netnummer
arm arm
aromatherapy
aromatherapie
around rond
arrivals (airport)
aankomst
arrive arriveren
art gallery
kunstgalerie
arthritis artritis
ashtray asbak
ask vragen
aspirin aspirine
assistance hulp
asthma astma
at (time) om;
(place) op
ATM geldautomaat
attack aanval
attractive
aantrekkelijk
audio guide
audiogids
aunt tante
Australia
Australië
authentic
authentiek
authenticity
echtheid
automatic (car)
automaat
available (seat)
vrij; (general)
beschikbaar
away adv weg
awful afschuwelijk

B

baby baby
baby bottle zuigfles
baby food babyvoeding
baby wipes babydoekjes
babysitter oppas
back (body part) rug; **(not front)** achterkant
backache rugpijn
backpack rugzak
bad slecht
bag tas
baggage [BE] bagage
baggage claim bagageafhaalruimte
bake bakken
bakery bakker
balcony balkon
ball bal
ballet ballet
band band
bandage (small) pleister; **(large)** verband
bank bank
bank charges bankkosten
bar bar
barber herenkapper
bargain koopje
barrier barrière
baseball honkbal
basement kelder
basket mand
basketball basketbal
bath bad

bathroom (bath/shower) badkamer; **(restroom)** toilet
battery (general) batterij; **(car)** accu
battlesite slagveld
be zijn
beach strand
beautiful mooi
because omdat
become worden
bed bed
bed and breakfast logies en ontbijt
bedding beddengoed
bedroom slaapkamer
before voor
begin beginnen
beginner beginner
behind achter
Belgium België
belong toebehoren
belt riem
bet wedden
between tussen
beware oppassen
bib slabbetje
bicycle fiets
big groot
bike path fietspad
bikini bikini
bill n rekening
binoculars verrekijker
bird vogel
birthday verjaardag
bite (general) beet; **(insect)** beet; v bijten

bitter bitter
bizarre bizar
bladder blaas
blanket deken
bleach bleekmiddel
bleed bloeden
blister blaar
blocked (drain) verstopt; **(road)** versperd
blood bloed
blood group bloedgroep
blood pressure bloeddruk
blouse bloes
blow dry föhnen
blue blauw
board v boarden
boarding card instapkaart
boat trip boottocht
bone bot
book boek
bookstore boekwinkel
boots laarzen
boring saai
born geboren
borrow lenen
botanical garden botanische tuin
bother v lastigvallen
bottle fles
bottle opener flesopener
boulevard boulevard
bowel darm
bowl kom
box doos
boxing boksen

boy jongen
boyfriend vriend
bra beha
bracelet armband
brake rem
break v breken
break down (car) pech hebben; **(appliance)** defect raken
breakfast ontbijt
breast borst
breastfeed borst geven
breathe ademhalen
bridge brug
bring brengen
British n Britten; adj Brits
brochure brochure
broken (body part or thing) gebroken; **(thing)** kapot
bronchitis bronchitis
brooch broche
broom bezem
bruise blauwe plek
bucket emmer
bug insect
building gebouw
build v bouwen
bulletin board mededelingenbord
burn brandwond
bus bus
bus lane busbaan
bus route busroute
bus shelter bushokje
bus station busstation
bus stop bushalte

bus ticket
strippenkaart
business zaken
business card
visitekaartje
business center
bedrijvencomplex
business class
businessclass
business district
zakendistrict
busy druk
but maar
butane gas
butagas
butcher slager
button knoop
buy kopen
by (near) bij;
(time) niet
later dan
**bye (also used
at arrival)**
dag; **(only at
departure)** tot
ziens

C

cabin hut
cafe café
calendar kalender
call n gesprek;
(phone) v bellen;
(name) v heten
calorie calorie
camera fototoestel
camp v kamperen
campsite camping
can (may) mogen;
(be able) kunnen
can opener
blikopener
Canada Canada
canal (general)

kanaal;
(in city) gracht
cancel annuleren
cancer kanker
candle kaars
canoeing
kanovaren
cap (hat) pet;
(dental) kroon
**capsule
(medication)**
capsule
car (vehicle)
auto; **(train
compartment)**
wagon
car deck (ferry)
autodek
car hire [BE]
autoverhuurbedrijf
car park [BE]
parkeerplaats
car rental
autoverhuurbedrijf
car seat kinderzitje
card kaart
careful voorzichtig
carpet tapijt
carry-on luggage
handbagage
cart wagentje
carton doos
cash adv contant;
v verzilveren
cash register
kassa
casino casino
castle kasteel
catch pakken;
(bus) nemen
cathedral
kathedraal
caution oppassen
cave grot

CD cd
CD player cd-
speler
**cell phone
(informal)**
mobiel; **(formal)**
mobiele telefoon
cemetery
begraafplaats
ceramics keramiek
certificate
certificaat
change (money)
n wisselgeld;
(buses)
v overstappen;
(money) v
wisselen;
(reservation)
v veranderen;
(baby)
v verschonen
charcoal houtskool
charge n prijs;
v berekenen
cheap goedkoop
check n rekening;
v checken
check in inchecken
check out (hotel)
uitchecken
checking account
betaalrekening
cheers proost
chemical toilet
chemisch toilet
**chemist [BE] (with
prescriptions)**
apotheek;
**(without
prescriptions)**
drogisterij
cheque [BE]
rekening

chest borstkas
child kind
child seat
kinderstoeltje
child's cot [BE]
wieg
children's clothing
kinderkleding
children's menu
kindermenu
children's portion
kinderportie
choose selecteren
church kerk
cigarette sigaret
cigar sigaar
cinema [BE]
bioscoop
class klas
clean schoon
cleaning supplies
schoonmaak-
middelen
clearance
opruiming
cliff klif
cling film [BE]
huishoudfolie
clinic kliniek
clock klok
clog n klomp
close adv dichtbij;
v sluiten
clothing store
kledingwinkel
cloudy bewolkt
club club
coast kust
coat jas
coat check
garderobe
coat hanger
kleerhanger
code code

coin munt
cold (chilly) koud;
  (flu) verkoudheid
collapse instorten
colleague collega
collect ophalen
collection (mail)
  lichting
color kleur
comb kam
come komen
commission
  commissie
compact compact
company
  (business)
  bedrijf;
  (companionship)
  gezelschap
compartment
  (train) coupé
computer
  computer
concert concert
concert hall
  concertgebouw
concession
  concessie
concussion
  hersenschudding
conditioner
  conditioner
condom condoom
conductor dirigent
conference
  conferentie
confirm bevestigen
congratulations
  gefeliciteerd
connect verbinding
  maken
connection
  verbinding
conscious bewust

conservation
  area beschermd
  natuurgebied
constant constant
constipation
  constipatie
consulate
  consulaat
consult raadplegen
contact bereiken
contact lens
  contactlens
contact lens
  solution contact-
  lensvloeistof
contagious
  besmettelijk
contain bevatten
contemporary
  modern
contest wedstrijd
continuous
  doorlopend
contraceptive
  voorbehoeds-
  middel
contribution
  bijdrage
control controle
convention
  congres
convention hall
  congresgebouw
cook n kok; v
  koken
cooker [BE]
  fornuis
cooking (cuisine)
  keuken
cooking facilities
  kookgelegenheid
cool (cold) koel;
  (nice) cool
copper koper

copy n kopie; v
  kopiëren
corkscrew
  kurkentrekker
corner hoek
correct correct
cosmetic
  cosmetisch
cost kosten
costume (local)
  klederdracht
cot ledikant
cottage
  vakantiehuisje
cotton katoen
cough n hoest;
  v hoesten
could kunnen
counter (shop)
  toonbank
country land
country code
  landnummer
courier koerier
course (meal)
  gang; (medication)
  kuur
courthouse
  rechtbank
cousin (male)
  neef; (female)
  nicht
cover charge
  couvert
craft shop
  handwerkwinkel
cramps kramp
credit card
  creditcard
crib wieg
cross n kruis;
  v oversteken
crossing
  overtocht

crosswalk
  zebrapad
crowded vol
crown (dental)
  kroon
cruise n cruise;
  v cruisen
crutches krukken
crystal kristal
cup kopje
currency valuta
currency
  exchange office
  geldwissel-
  kantoor
curtain gordijn
curve bocht
custom made op
  maat gemaakt
customer
  information
  klanteninformatie
customer service
  klantenservice
customs douane
customs declara-
  tion form
  douaneaangifte-
  formulier
cut n snijwond;
  v knippen
cute schattig
cycle route
  fietsroute
cycling fietsen
cycling race
  wielerwedstrijd

D

daily dagelijks
dairy zuivel
dairy products
  zuivelproducten
damage schade

damaged beschadigd

damp vochtig

dance *n* dans; *v* dansen

dance club discotheek

dangerous gevaarlijk

dark donker

date of birth geboortedatum

dawn dageraad

day dag

day trip dagtocht

dead end doodlopende weg

deaf doof

deck chair ligstoel

declare aangeven

decorative decoratief

decorative tile siertegel

deep diep

defrost ontdooien

degree graad

delay vertraging

delete verwijderen

Delft blue Delfts blauw

delicatessen delicatessen

delicious heerlijk

deliver (give birth) bevallen; **(bring)** afleveren

delivery levering

denim spijkerstof

dental floss floss

dental office tandartspraktijk

dentist tandarts

denture kunstgebit

deodorant deodorant

depart vertrekken

department store warenhuis

departure gate vertrekgate

departure lounge vertrekhal

departures vertrek

deposit *n* borgsom

describe beschrijven

destination bestemming

detail detail

detergent wasmiddel

detour omleiding

develop ontwikkelen

diabetes diabetes

diabetic *adj* diabetisch; *n* suikerpatiënt

dial (phone) *v* kiezen

diamond diamant

diaper luier

diarrhea diarree

diabetic suikerpatiënt

dice dobbelsteen

dictionary woordenboek

diesel diesel

diet dieet

difficult moeilijk

digital digitaal

dine dineren

dining car restauratiewagen

dining room eetkamer

dinner avondeten

direct *adj* rechtstreeks; *v* de weg wijzen

direction richting

directions (map) aanwijzingen

directory (phone) telefoonboek

dirty vies

disabled gehandicapt

disconnect verbinding verbreken

discount korting

discount store discountzaak

dish (plate) bord; **(food)** gerecht

dishwasher afwasmachine

dishwashing liquid afwasmiddel

dislocate ontwrichten

display case vitrine

disposable wegwerpbaar

dissolve oplossen

distance afstand

disturb storen

dive duiken

diving equipment duikapparatuur

divorce scheiden

dizzy duizelig

do doen

dock dok

doctor dokter

dog hond

doll pop

dollar (U.S.) dollar

domestic binnenlands

donation gift

door deur

dosage dosering

double dubbel

double room tweepersoonskamer

downstairs beneden

downtown stadscentrum

dozen dozijn

dress *n* jurk; *v* aankleden

dress code kledingvoorschriften

drink *n* drankje; *v* drinken

drip druppelen

drive rijden

driver chauffeur

driver's license rijbewijs

drop (medicine) druppel

drown verdrinken

drowsy suf

drowsiness sufheid

drugstore drogisterij

drunk dronken

dry droog

dry clean stomen

dry cleaner stomerij

dubbed nagesynchroniseerd

dummy [BE] fopspeen

during tijdens

Dutch (language)
Nederlands;
(people)
Nederlanders
duty (tax) accijns
duty-free
belastingvrij

E

ear oor
ear drops
oordruppels
earache oorpijn
early vroeg
earrings oorbellen
east oost
easy makkelijk
eat eten
**economy class
(general)**
economy class;
(train) tweede
klas
electrical outlet
stopcontact
electronic
elektronisch
elevator n lift
e-mail e-mail
e-mail address
e-mailadres
embassy
ambassade
emerald smaragd
emergency
noodgeval
emergency brake
noodrem
emergency exit
nooduitgang
emergency service
hulpdienst
empty adj leeg;
v leegmaken

end n einde; v
aflopen
**engaged
(marriage)**
verloofd
England Engeland
English Engels
English-speaking
Engelstalig
engrave graveren
enjoy leuk
vinden
enlarge vergroten
enough genoeg
**entertainment
guide** uitgids
entrance ingang
entrance fee
toegangsprijs
**entrance ramp
(highway)** oprit
snelweg
entry ingang
entry visa
inreisvisum
envelope envelop
epileptic
epileptisch
**equipment
(clothing)**
uitrusting;
(machine)
apparatuur
error fout
escalator roltrap
essential
essentieel
e-ticket e-ticket
euro euro
Eurocheque
Eurocheque
evening avond
event evenement
every elk

exact exact
examination
onderzoek
example voorbeeld
except
uitgezonderd
excess luggage
overbagage
exchange (general)
ruilen; **(money)**
wisselen
exchange rate
wisselkoers
excursion
excursie
exhausted
uitgeput
exit (door)
uitgang;
(highway)
afslag
exit ramp afrit
expensive duur
experience
ervaring
expiration date
vervaldatum
expose
blootstellen
express mail per
expres
extension (phone)
toestel
extra (additional)
extra
extract v
onttrekken
eye oog
eyebrow
wenkbrauw

F

fabric stof
face gezicht

facial n gezichtsbe-
handeling
facilities
faciliteiten
factor factor
faint adj zwak;
v flauwvallen
fall v vallen
family (immediate)
gezin; **(relatives)**
familie
famous beroemd
fan n ventilator
far ver
far-sighted
verziend
farm boerderij
fast (speedy)
snel; **(clock)**
loopt voor
fast food fastfood
faucet kraan
faulty defect
favorite favoriet
fax fax
fax machine
faxapparaat
fax number
faxnummer
feature kenmerk
feed voeden
feel voelen
female vrouwelijk
ferry veerboot
fever koorts
few weinig
fiancé verloofde
field weiland
fight n gevecht;
v vechten
fill vullen
fill out invullen
fill up opvullen
filling vulling

film (movie)
  film; **(camera)**
  fotorolletje
filter filter
find vinden
fine (good) goed;
  (well) prima;
  (police) boete
finger vinger
fire (campfire)
  kampvuur;
  (disaster) brand
fire alarm
  brandalarm
fire brigade [BE]
  brandweer
fire department
  brandweer
fire door branddeur
fire escape
  nooduitgang
fire exit brandtrap
fire extinguisher
  brandblusser
first eerst
first class eerste
  klas
fishing v vissen
fit passen
fitting room
  paskamer
fix (repair)
  repareren
flash flits
flashlight
  zaklantaarn
flavor smaak
flea market
  vlooienmarkt
flight vlucht
**flight attendant
  (male) steward;**
  (female)
  stewardess

flight number
  vluchtnummer
floor (level)
  verdieping
florist
  bloemenwinkel
flower bloem
flu griep
flush doorspoelen
fly n vlieg; v vliegen
fog mist
follow volgen
food voedsel
food poisoning
  voedsel-
  vergiftiging
foot voet
footpath [BE]
  voetpad
football [BE]
  voetbal
for voor
for sale te koop
foreign buitenlands
forest bos
forget vergeten
fork vork
form n formulier
formal dress
  avondkleding
formula (baby)
  flesvoeding
fountain fontein
fracture breuk
frame (glasses)
  montuur
free (available)
  vrij
free of charge
  gratis
freeze bevriezen
freezer diepvriezer
frequent adj vaak
fresh vers

friend vriend
from (general)van;
  (destination)
  uit
front voorkant
frying pan
  koekenpan
fuel (gas) benzine
full vol
fun plezier
funny grappig
furniture meubels
fuse zekering
fuse box
  zekeringkast

G

gallery galerie
**game
  (competition)**
  wedstrijd;
  (tennis) game;
  (toy) spelletje
garage garage
garbage bag
  vuilniszak
garden tuin
gas (gasoline)
  benzine
gas station
  benzinestation
gas tank
  benzinetank
gate (airport)
  gate; **(general)**
  hek
gauze gaas
gear versnelling
genuine echt
get (receive)
  krijgen
get off (bus)
  uitstappen
gift cadeau

gift store
  cadeauwinkel
girl meisje
girlfriend vriendin
give geven
glass (drinking)
  glas
glasses (optical)
  bril
gloves
  handschoenen
gluten gluten
go gaan
goggles duikbril
gold goud
golf golf
golf club golfstok
golf course
  golfbaan
good goed
goodbye dag
gram gram
grass gras
great prima
Great Britain
  Groot-Brittannië
green groen
greengrocer [BE]
  groenteman
groundcloth
  grondzeil
groundsheet [BE]
  grondzeil
group groep
guarantee
  garantie
guesthouse
  pension
guide (tour) gids
guide book gids
guide dog
  geleidehond
guided tour
  rondleiding

guided walk
begeleide
wandeling
guitar gitaar
gym fitnessruimte
gynecologist
gynaecoloog

H

hair haar
hairbrush borstel
hairdresser
dameskapper
halal halal
half n helft; adj
halve
hammer hamer
hand hand
hand luggage
handbagage
hand washable
met de hand
wassen
handbag [BE]
handtas
handicapped
gehandicapt
handicrafts
ambachten
handkerchief
zakdoek
hanger
klerenhanger
hangover kater
happen gebeuren
happy blij
harbor haven
hard (tough)
  hard; (difficult)
moeilijk
hardware store
ijzerwarenwinkel
hat hoed
have hebben

hay fever
hooikoorts
head hoofd
headache
hoofdpijn
health gezondheid
health food
reformproducten
health food store
reformwinkel
health insurance
ziektekostenverze-
kering
hear v horen
hearing aid
gehoorapparaat
hearing impaired
slechthorend
heart hart
heart attack
hartaanval
heart condition
hartkwaal
heat verwarming
heating [BE]
verwarming
heavy zwaar
height (person)
lengte; (general)
hoogte
hello hallo
helmet helm
help helpen
her haar
here hier
hi hallo
high hoog
highchair
kinderstoel
highway snelweg
hiking wandelen
hiking gear
wandeluitrusting
hill heuvel

hire huren
historical
historisch
hobby hobby
hold (general)
vasthouden;
(phone) aan de
lijn blijven
hole gat
holiday [BE]
vakantie
home (place)
thuis; **(direction)**
naar huis
homemade
zelfgemaakt
honeymoon
huwelijksreis
horn claxon
horse paard
horseback riding
paardrijden
horsetrack
paardenrenbaan
hospital
ziekenhuis
hot heet
hotel hotel
hour uur
house huis
how hoe
how much
hoeveel
how many
hoeveel
hug omhelzen
hunger honger
hungry hongerig
hunt jagen
hurry n haast;
v haasten
hurt n pijn; v pijn
hebben
husband man

I

I ik
ibuprofen
ibuprofen
ice-cream parlor
ijssalon
ice hockey
ijshockey
ice skating
schaatsen
identification
legitimatiebewijs
ill [BE] ziek
illegal illegaal
imitation imitatie
important
belangrijk
improve verbeteren
in in
incline helling
include bevatten
indigestion
indigestie
indoor pool
binnenbad
inexpensive
goedkoop
infect ontsteken
infection infectie
inflammation
ontsteking
informal
informeel
information
(general)
informatie;
(phone inquiry)
inlichtingen
information desk
informatiebalie
injection injectie
injure verwonden
innocent
onschuldig

insect insect
insect bite insectenbeet
insect repellent insectenspray
insert (ATM) invoeren
inside binnen
insist aandringen
insomnia slapeloosheid
instant messenger instant messenger
instead of in plaats van
instructions gebruiks- aanwijzing
instructor instructeur
insulin insuline
insurance verzekering
insurance card verzekeringsbewijs
insurance certificate [BE] verzekerings- bewijs
insurance claim schadeclaim
interest (hobby) interesse
interference storing
intermission pauze
international internationaal
International Student Card Internationale Studentenkaart
internet internet

internet cafe internetcafé
internet service internetverbinding
interpreter tolk
intersection kruispunt
into naar
introduce (person) voorstellen
invite uitnodigen
iodine jodium
Ireland Ierland
iron n strijkijzer
is is
itch jeuk
item ding
itemized gespecificeerd

J

jacket jasje
jar pot
jaw kaak
jeans spijkerbroek
jet lag jetlag
jet-ski jetski
jeweler juwelier
jewelry sieraden
job baan
join meedoen
joint adj gezamenlijk; n gewricht
joke grap
journey reis

K

keep houden
keep out verboden toegang
key sleutel
key card sleutelkaart

key ring sleutelring
kiddie pool kinderbadje
kidney nier
kilo kilo
kilometer kilometer
kind (pleasant) aardig; **(type)** soort
kiss v kussen
kitchen keuken
knee knie
knife mes
knock kloppen
know kennen
kosher koosjer

L

label label
lace kant
lactose intolerant lactose-intolerant
ladder ladder
lake meer
lamp lamp
land n land; v landen
lane (traffic) rijstrook; **(path)** laantje
language course taalcursus
large groot
last (end) adj laatst; **(previous)** adj vorige; **(keep)** v meegaan
late (delayed) vertraagd
launderette [BE] wasserette

laundromat wasserette
laundry service wasserij
laundry facilities wasmachines
lawyer advocaat
laxative laxerend middel
lead (road) gaan naar
leader (group) groepsleider
leak lekken
learn leren
leather leer
leave (depart) vertrekken; **(deposit)** betalen; **(forget something)** vergeten
left links
left-luggage office [BE] bagagedepot
leg (body part) been
legal legaal
lend lenen
length lengte
lens lens
lens cap lensdop
less minder
lesson les
let laten
letter brief
level adj gelijk; n verdieping
library biblio- theek
life leven
life boat reddingsboot

life guard (pool)
badmeester;
(beach)
strandmeester
life jacket
reddingsvest
lift [BE] lift
light licht
lightbulb
gloeilamp
lighthouse
vuurtoren
lighter *adj* lichter;
n aansteker
line lijn
linen linnen
lip lip
lipstick lippenstift
liquor store
slijter
liter liter
little klein
live wonen
liver lever
living room
woonkamer
loafers instappers
**lobby (theater,
hotel)** hal
local plaatselijk
lock *n* slot; *v*
afsluiten
log on inloggen
log off uitloggen
long lang
long-distance bus
touringcar
long-sighted [BE]
verziend
look *n* stijl; *v* kijken
loose los
lorry [BE]
vrachtauto
lose verliezen

lost (misplaced)
verloren;
(direction)
verdwaald
lost-and-found
gevonden
voorwerpen
**lost property
office** [BE]
gevonden
voorwerpen
lottery loterij
loud (general)
luid; **(voice)**
hard
love *n* liefde;
(general) v
dol zijn op;
(romantic)
v houden van
low laag
luggage bagage
luggage cart
bagagewagentje
**luggage
trolley** [BE]
bagagewagentje
lump gezwel
lunch lunch
lung long

M

machine washable
in de machine
wassen
madam mevrouw
magazine
tijdschrift
magnificent
magnifiek
mail *n* post; *v*
posten
mailbox brievenbus
main grootste

make-up make-up
male mannelijk
mall
winkelcentrum
mallet houten
hamer
man man
manager manager
mandatory
verplicht
manicure manicure
many veel
map kaart
market markt
marry trouwen
mascara mascara
mask masker
mass mis
massage
massage
matches lucifers
matinee matinee
mattress matras
maybe misschien
meal maaltijd
mean *v* betekenen
measure meten
measurement
afmeting
measuring cup
maatbeker
measuring spoon
maatlepel
mechanic
monteur
medication
medicijn
medicine
geneesmiddel
meet ontmoeten
meeting
vergadering
meeting room
vergaderruimte

meeting place
ontmoetingsplaats
member lid
memorial
gedenkteken
memory card
geheugenkaart
mend (clothes)
verstellen
menstrual cramps
menstruatiepijn
menu menukaart
merge (traffic)
invoegen
message bericht
metal metaal
microwave (oven)
magnetron
midday [BE] twaalf
uur 's middags
midnight
middernacht
migraine migraine
mini-bar minibar
minute minuut
mirror spiegel
missing kwijt
mistake fout
mobile home
camper
mobile phone
[BE] **(informal)**
mobiel; **(formal)**
mobiele telefoon
**moisturizer
(cream)**
vochtinbrengende
crème
money geld
money order
postwissel
month maand
mop dweil
moped brommer

more meer
morning ochtend
mosque moskee
mosquito bite
muggenbeet
motion sickness
reisziekte
motor motor
motor boat
motorboot
motorcycle
motorfiets
motorway [BE]
snelweg
mountain berg
mountain bike
mountainbike
moustache snor
mouth mond
move (general)
bewegen;
(relocate)
verhuizen
movie film
movie theater
bioscoop
Mr. De heer (Dhr.);
meneer
Mrs. Mevrouw
(Mevr.)
much veel
mugging bero-
ving
mug mok
muscle spier
museum museum
music muziek
must moeten

N

nail nagel
nail file nagelvijl
nail salon
nagelsalon

name naam
napkin servet
nappy [BE] luier
narrow smal
national nationaal
nationality
nationaliteit
native inwoner
nature natuur
nature reserve
natuurreservaat
nature trail
natuurpad
nausea
misselijkheid
nauseous
misselijk
near dichtbij
nearby in de
buurt
nearest
dichtstbijzijnde
near-sighted
bijziend
necessary nodig
neck nek
necklace
halsketting
need v nodig
hebben
network netwerk
never nooit
new nieuw
New Zealand
Nieuw-Zeeland
news nieuws
news agent [BE]
kiosk
newspaper krant
newsstand kiosk
next volgende
next to naast
nice fijn
night nacht

night club
nachtclub
no (denial) nee;
(prohibition)
niet
no parking
parkeerverbod
noisy lawaaierig
non-EU citizens
niet-EU-
ingezetenen
non-smoking
niet-roken
non-stop non-stop
noon twaalf uur 's
middags
normal normaal
north noord
nose neus
not niet
nothing niets
notify informeren
now nu
number nummer
nurse verpleegster
nylon nylon

O

o'clock uur
office kantoor
office hours
kantooruren
office supplies
kantoorbenodigd-
heden
off-licence [BE]
slijter
off-peak (ticket)
daluren
office kantoor
often vaak
oil olie
OK oké
old oud

on op
once één keer
one-way (traffic)
eenrichtings-
verkeer
one-way ticket
enkeltje
only slechts
open adj
open; **(shop)**
v opengaan;
(window)
v opendoen
opening hours [BE]
openingstijden
opera opera
operation operatie
opposite tegenover
opticien opticiën
or of
orally oraal
orchestra orkest
order bestellen
organize
organiseren
original origineel
out uit
outdoor adj
openlucht
outdoor pool
buitenbad
outside buiten
oval ovaal
oven oven
over (more than)
meer dan
overcharged
teveel betaald
overheat
oververhit worden
overlook
uitkijkpunt
overnight in één
nacht

owe verschuldigd zijn
own adj eigen; v bezitten
owner eigenaar
oxygen zuurstof

P

pacifier fopspeen
pack inpakken
package pakje
paddling pool [BE] kinderzwembad
padlock hangslot
pail emmer
pain pijn
paint v verven
painting schilderij
pair paar
pajamas pyjama
palace paleis
palpitations hartkloppingen
panorama panorama
pants lange broek
panty hose panty
paper towel keukenpapier
paracetamol [BE] paracetamol
paralysis verlamming
parcel [BE] pak
parents ouders
park n park; v parkeren
parking garage parkeergarage
parking lot parkeerplaats
parking meter parkeermeter

parking ticket parkeerbon
partner partner
part time parttime
party (social) feestje
pass (a place) langskomen; **(traffic)** inhalen
passenger passagier
passport paspoort
password wachtwoord
pastry store banketbakker
patient adj geduldig; n patiënt
pavement [BE] stoep
pay phone telefoonzuil
pay betalen
payment betaling
pearl parel
pedestrian voetganger
pedestrian crossing voetgangersoversteekplaats
pedestrian zone verkeersvrij gebied
pediatrician kinderarts
pedicure pedicure
peg wasknijper
pen pen
penicillin penicilline
per per
performance voorstelling

perhaps misschien
period (general) periode; **(menstrual)** menstruatie
person persoon
petite tenger
petrol [BE] benzine
petrol station [BE] benzinestation
pewter tin
pharmacy apotheek
phone n telefoon; v telefoneren
phone call telefoongesprek
phone card telefoonkaart
phone directory telefoongids
phone number telefoonnummer
photocopy n kopie; v kopiëren
photograph foto
photography fotografie
phrase zinsnede
phrase book taalgids
pick up v ophalen
picnic picknick
picnic area picknickplaats
piece stuk
pill pil
pillow kussen
PIN PIN
pipe (smoking) pijp
pizzeria pizzeria
place plaats
plane vliegtuig

plan plan
plaster [BE] pleister
plastic plastic
plastic wrap huishoudfolie
plate bord
platform spoor
platinum platina
play n toneelstuk; v spelen
playground speeltuin
playpen babybox
pleasant prettig
please alstublieft
plug plug
plunger ontstopper
pneumonia longontsteking
poison gif
police politie
police report proces-verbaal
police station politiebureau
pollen count stuifmeelgehalte
polyester polyester
pond vijver
pool zwembad
popular populair
porcelain porselein
port (harbor) haven
porter kruier
portion portie
post [BE] n post; v versturen
post office postkantoor
postage posttarief

postbox [BE]
brievenbus
postcard
ansichtkaart
pot pot
pottery aardewerk
pound pond
pound sterling
Britse pond
power (electricity)
stroom
practice praktijk
pregnant zwanger
premium (gas)
super
prepaid phone card
prepaidkaart
prescription
recept
present n cadeau;
v geven
press persen
pretty mooi
price prijs
print afdrukken
prison gevangenis
private particulier
produce store
groentewinkel
profession beroep
problem probleem
prohibited
verboden
program
programma
pronounce
uitspreken
pub pub
public n publiek;
adj openbaar
pull trekken
pump pomp
pure zuiver
purpose doel

purse (handbag)
handtas
push duwen
pushchair [BE]
kinderwagen
put neerzetten

Q

quality kwaliteit
quarter kwart
queue [BE] n rij; v
in de rij staan
quick snel
quiet rustig

R

racetrack circuit
racket (tennis)
racket
railroad crossing
overweg
**railway station
[BE]** station
rain n regen; v
regenen
raincoat regenjas
rape verkrachting
rapids
stroomversnelling
rash uitslag
razor
scheerapparaat
reach bereiken
reaction reactie
read lezen
ready klaar
real (genuine)
echt
receipt (in shop)
bon; (formal)
kwitantie
receive ontvangen
reception (desk)
receptie

receptionist
receptionist
recommend
aanbevelen
reduce
verminderen
reduction korting
refrigerator
koelkast
refund n
terugbetaling;
v terugbetalen
region streek
registered mail
aangetekende
post
registration form
inschrijfformulier
regular normaal
relationship
relatie
reliable
betrouwbaar
religion godsdienst
remember (recall)
herinneren;
(not forget)
onthouden
remove
verwijderen
renovation
renovatie
rent n huur; v huren
rental car
huurauto
repair repareren
repeat herhalen
replace vervangen
replacement part
vervangings-
onderdeel
report n rapport;
v melden
required vereist

reservation
reservering
reservation desk
reserveringsbalie
reserve reserveren
reservoir reservoir
responsibility
verantwoor-
delijkheid
rest rusten
rest area
rustgebied
restaurant
restaurant
restroom toilet
retired
gepensioneerd
return ticket [BE]
retourtje
right (correct)
juist; **(direction)**
rechts
ring ring
river rivier
road weg
road map
wegenkaart
roadwork
wegwerk-
zaamheden
rob beroven
robbery beroving
rock rots
romantic
romantisch
roof dak
room kamer
room service
roomservice
rope touw
rose roos
round rond
round-trip ticket
retourtje

route route
row roeien
rowboat roeiboot
rubbish [BE]
 vuilnis
rude onbeleefd
ruins ruine
rush haasten

S

safe adj veilig;
 n kluis
safety veiligheid
safety pin
 veiligheidsspeld
sale opruiming
sales tax BTW
same hetzelfde
sand zand
sandals sandalen
sanitary napkin
 maandverband
sanitary pad [BE]
 maandverband
satin satijn
saucepan steelpan
sauna sauna
save (computer)
 opslaan
savings account
 spaarrekening
say zeggen
scarf sjaal
scissors schaar
Scotland
 Schotland
screwdriver
 schroevendraaier
sea zee
seasick zeeziek
season ticket
 abonnement
seat (on train,
 etc.) plaats

seat belt
 veiligheidsgordel
sedative
 kalmerend middel
see zien
self-service
 zelfbediening
sell verkopen
seminar seminar
send versturen
senior citizen
 oudere
separated uit
 elkaar
separate apart
serious ernstig
serve opdienen
service (church)
 kerkdienst;
 (restaurant)
 bediening
service charge
 bedieningsgeld
service included
 bediening
 inbegrepen
set menu
 dagmenu
sew naaien
sex seks
shadow schaduw
shallow ondiep
shampoo
 shampoo
shape vorm
share delen
sharp scherp
shave scheren
shaving brush
 scheerkwast
shaving cream
 scheerzeep
sheet (bed) laken
ship schip

shirt (men's)
 overhemd
shock schok
shoe schoen
shoe repair
 schoenmaker
shoe store
 schoenenwinkel
shop assistant
 winkelbediende
shopping
 n boodschappen;
 v winkelen
shopping basket
 winkelmandje
shopping
centre [BE]
 winkelcentrum
shopping mall
 winkelcentrum
shopping cart
 winkelwagentje
shopping
trolley [BE]
 winkelwagentje
short kort
short-sighted [BE]
 bijziend
shorts korte broek
shoulder schouder
shovel schep
show tonen
shower douche
shut v sluiten
shutter luik
sick (general) ziek;
 (nauseous)
 misselijk
side effect
 bijwerking
sidewalk stoep
sight (attraction)
 bezienswaardig-
 heid

sightseeing tour
 toeristische
 rondrit
sign (road)
 n verkeersbord;
 (place signature)
 v tekenen
silk zijde
silver zilver
single (person)
 single
single ticket [BE]
 (travel) enkeltje
single room
 eenpersoons-
 kamer
sink (bathroom)
 wastafel;
 (kitchen)
 gootsteen
sit zitten
site plaats
size maat
skating rink
 ijsbaan
skin huid
skirt rok
sleep slapen
sleeping bag
 slaapzak
sleeping car
 slaapwagen
sleeping pill
 slaappil
sleeve mouw
slice plak
slippers pantoffels
slow langzaam
small klein
smell geur
smoke roken
smoking area
 rokerszone
snack snack

snack bar
snackbar
sneakers
gymschoenen
snorkle snorkelen
snow n sneeuw;
v sneeuwen
soap zeep
soccer voetbal
socket stopcontact
socks sokken
sold out
uitverkocht
some enkele
someone iemand
something iets
sometimes soms
somewhere ergens
soon gauw
soother [BE]
fopspeen
sore pijnlijk
sore throat
keelpijn
sorry sorry
south zuid
souvenir souvenir
souvenir guide
souvenirgids
souvenir store
souvenirwinkel
spa kuuroord
space ruimte
spare extra
spatula spatel
speak spreken
special speciaal
specialist
specialist
specimen monster
speed snelheid
speed limit
snelheidslimiet
spell v spellen

spend uitgeven
sponge spons
spoon lepel
sport sport
sporting goods
store sportwinkel
sports club
sportvereniging
spot (place, site)
plaats
spouse (male)
echtgenoot;
(female)
echtgenote
sprain n
verstuiking;
v verstuiken
square vierkant
stadium stadion
staff personeel
stainless steel
roestvrij staal
stairs trap
stamp n postzegel;
v stempelen
stand staan
standard
standaard
standby ticket
standby-ticket
start (general)
beginnen;
(car, etc.) starten
statue standbeeld
stay n verblijf;
(remain) v
blijven;
(overnight)
v logeren
steal stelen
steel staal
steep steil
sterilizing solution
steriele oplossing

sterling silver
sterling zilver
stiff stijf
still nog
stolen gestolen
stomach maag
stomachache
maagpijn
stop n halte; v
stoppen
store winkel
store directory
[BE]
winkelplattegrond
store guide
winkelplatte-
grond
stove fornuis
straight recht
stream beekje
street straat
stroller
kinderwagen
strong sterk
student student
study studeren
stunning
verbluffend
style n stijl; v
stylen
subtitled
ondertiteld
suburb buitenwijk
subway metro
subway map
metrokaart
subway station
metrostation
suggest
voorstellen
suit pak
suitable geschikt
suitcase koffer
sun zon

sunbathe
zonnebaden
sunblock sunblock
sunburn
zonnebrand
sunglasses
zonnebril
sunshade [BE]
parasol
sunscreen
zonnebrandcrème
suntan lotion
zonnebrandcrème
super (petrol) [BE]
super
superb
voortreffelijk
supermarket
supermarkt
supervision
toezicht
suppository zetpil
surcharge toeslag
sure zeker
surfboard
surfplank
swallow
doorslikken
sweater trui
sweatshirt
sweatshirt
sweep vegen
sweet zoet
swelling zwelling
swim zwemmen
swimsuit zwempak
swimming pool
zwembad
swimming trunks
zwembroek
swollen opgezet
symbol symbool
symptom
symptoom

synagogue
synagoge
synthetic
synthetisch

T
T-shirt T-shirt
TV tv
table tafel
tablet tablet
take (general)
nemen; **(carry)**
meenemen;
(medicine)
innemen; **(time)**
duren
take off (plane)
opstijgen;
(shoes) uitdoen
talk praten
tall lang
tampon tampon
tap [BE] kraan
taste *n* smaak;
v proeven
taxi taxi
taxi rank [BE]
taxistandplaats
taxi stand
taxistandplaats
teaspoon theelepel
team team
tear (muscle)
scheuren
tear off afscheuren
telephone *n*
telefoon;
v telefoneren
telephone booth
telefoonzuil
telephone call
telefoongesprek
telephone number
telefoonnummer

tell vertellen
temperature
temperatuur
tennis tennis
tennis court
tennisbaan
tent tent
tent peg tentharing
tent pole tentstok
terminal terminal
terrible vreselijk
text *n* tekst
text messaging
sms'en
thank danken
that dat
theater theater
theft diefstal
then (time) dan
there daar
thermometer
thermometer
thermos
thermosfles
these deze
thick dik
thief dief
thigh dij
thin dun
thing ding
think denken
thirsty dorstig
this dit
those die
throat keel
through door
thumb duim
ticket kaartje
ticket inspector
conducteur
ticket office loket
tie *n* stropdas
tight krap
tile tegel

time tijd
timetable [BE]
dienstregeling
tip fooi
tire band
tired moe
tissue tissue
to (place) naar
tobacco tabak
tobacconist
sigarenwinkel
today vandaag
toe teen
toilet [BE] toilet
toilet paper
toiletpapier
toll tol
toll booth tolhuisje
toll road tolweg
tomorrow morgen
tongue tong
tonight vanavond
too te
tooth tand
toothache kiespijn
toothbrush
tandenborstel
toothpaste
tandpasta
top bovenkant
torn gescheurd
tour excursie
tour guide
reisgids
tourist toerist
tourist office VVV-
kantoor
tournament
toernooi
tow truck
takelwagen
towel handdoek
tower toren
town stad

town hall stadhuis
town map
stadsplattegrond
town square
stadsplein
toy speelgoed
toy store
speelgoedwinkel
traditional
traditioneel
traffic verkeer
traffic circle
rotonde
traffic jam file
traffic light
stoplicht
traffic offence [BE]
verkeersover-
treding
traffic violation
verkeersover-
treding
trail wandelpad
trailer
aanhangwagen
train trein
train station
station
tram tram
transfer
overstappen
transport vervoer
translate vertalen
translation
vertaling
translator vertaler
trash vuilnis
trash can
vuilnisbak
travel reizen
travel agency
reisbureau
travel sickness
reisziekte

traveler's check reischeque
traveller's cheque [BE] reischeque
tray plateau
treatment behandeling
tree boom
trim bijknippen
trip reis
trolley wagentje
trousers [BE] lange broek
truck vrachtwagen
true waar
try on (clothes) passen
tumor tumor
tunnel tunnel
turn (traffic) keren
turn down (volume, heat) lager zetten
turn off uitzetten
turn on aanzetten
turn up hoger zetten
tweezers pincet
twist (ankle) verstuiken
typical typisch

U

U.K. Groot-Brittannië
U.S. Verenigde Staten
ugly lelijk
ulcer zweer
umbrella paraplu
unconscious bewusteloos
under onder
underground station [BE] metrostation

understand begrijpen
unemployed werkeloos
units (phone card) eenheden
until tot
upstairs boven
urgent dringend
use n gebruik; v gebruiken
username gebruikersnaam

V

vacant vrij
vacation vakantie
vacuum cleaner stofzuiger
valet service parkeerdienst
valid geldig
validate (general) bevestigen; **(ticket)** afstempelen
valuable waardevol
value waarde
VAT [BE] BTW
vegan veganist
vegetarian n vegetariër; adj vegetarisch
vehicle voertuig
vein ader
version versie
very heel
video game videospelletje
view uitzicht
viewpoint uitkijkpunt
village dorp

vineyard wijngaard
visa visum
visit n bezoek; v bezoeken
visiting hours bezoekuur
visually impaired slechtziend
volleyball volleybal
voltage voltage
vomit n braaksel; v overgeven

W

wait wachten
waiting room wachtkamer
waiter kelner
waitress kelnerin
wake (self) wakker worden; **(someone)** wakker maken
wake-up service wekdienst
Wales Wales
walk (general) lopen; **(on trail/ path)** wandelen
wall muur
wallet portemonnee
ward (hospital) afdeling
warm adj warm; v opwarmen
war memorial oorlogsmonument
warning waarschuwing
washable wasbaar
washing machine wasmachine

watch (timepiece) horloge
water water
water skis waterski's
waterfall waterval
waterproof waterdicht
wave golf
way weg
wear dragen
weather weer
weather forecast weerbericht
wedding huwelijk
week week
weekday weekdag
weekend weekend
weekend rate weekendtarief
weekly wekelijks
weigh wegen
weight gewicht
welcome welkom
west west
wetsuit duikerspak
what wat
wheelchair rolstoel
wheelchair ramp rolstoelopgang
when wanneer
where waar
which welke
while terwijl
who wie
whose van wie
why waarom
wide breed
wife vrouw
wildlife dieren in het wild
wind wind

windbreaker windjack
windmill molen
windscreen voorruit
windsurfing windsurfen
windy winderig
window (general) raam; **(shop)** etalage
window seat plaats bij het raam
wine wijn
wine list wijnkaart
wipe vegen

wireless draadloos
wish wens
with met
withdraw (money) opnemen
withdrawal (money) geldopname
within (time) binnen
without zonder
witness getuige
wood (forest) bos; **(material)** hout
wool wol

work (function) n werk v werken; **(operate)** bedienen
wrap v inpakken
write schrijven
wrong verkeerd

X

x-ray röntgenfoto

Y

yacht jacht
year jaar
yes ja
yesterday gisteren

yield (traffic) voorrang verlenen
you (sing. for.) u; **(sing. inf.)** jij; **(pl. for.)** u; **(pl. inf.)** jullie
young jong
youth jongeren
youth hostel jeugdherberg

Z

zebra crossing [BE] zebrapad
zero nul
zipper ritssluiting
zoo dierentuin

INDEX

Berlitz pocket guide

BRUSSELS

Eighth Edition 2018

Editor: Ros Walford
Author: Michele A. Berdy
Head of DTP and Pre-Press: Rebeka Davies
Picture Editor: Tom Smyth
Cartography Update: Carte
Update Production: Apa Digital
Photography Credits: 123RF 17; BCSC/
Daniel Fouss 40; Bigstock 92; Eric
Danheir/Visit Brussels 33; Glyn Genin/Apa
Publications 71, 72, 73; iStock 1, 4TC,
4MC, 4ML, 5T, 5MC, 5M, 5M, 7, 11, 15, 21,
23, 31, 34, 36, 44, 47, 57, 60, 63, 65, 67, 68,
74, 77, 79, 81, 82, 85, 95, 102; Julian Love/
Apa Publications 6R, 7R, 12, 28, 39, 42,
49, 51, 52, 54, 59, 86, 88, 90, 91, 101, 104;
Leonardo 6L; MIM/Visit Brussels 43;
Olivier van de Kerchove/Visit Brussels 96;
Paul Hermans 83; Public domain 18, 24;
Shutterstock 4TL, 5TC, 5MC, 98
Cover Picture: iStock

Distribution
UK, Ireland and Europe: Apa Publications
(UK) Ltd; sales@insightguides.com
United States and Canada: Ingram
Publisher Services; ips@ingramcontent.com
Australia and New Zealand: Woodslane;
info@woodslane.com.au
Southeast Asia: Apa Publications (SN) Pte;
singaporeoffice@insightguides.com
Worldwide: Apa Publications (UK) Ltd;
sales@insightguides.com

**Special Sales, Content Licensing
and CoPublishing**
Insight Guides can be purchased in bulk
quantities at discounted prices. We can
create special editions, personalised jackets
and corporate imprints tailored to your
needs. sales@insightguides.com;
www.insightguides.biz

All Rights Reserved
© 2018 Apa Digital (CH) AG and
Apa Publications (UK) Ltd

Printed in China by CTPS

M Métro / Metro

1 *Weststation* / Gare de l'Ouest - Stockel / *Stokkel*
2 Simonis - Elisabeth
5 Erasme / *Erasmus* - Hermann-Debroux
6 *Koning Boudewijn* / Roi Baudouin - Elisabeth

Terminus, *eindpunt*, Terminus

Accessible aux PMR avec aide, *toegankelijk voor PBM met hulp*
Accessible for PBM with assistance

T Tram / Tramway ● ● ● CHRONO ●

3 Esplanade - Churchill
4 Gare du Nord / *Noordstation* - Stalle 🅿
7 Heizel / *Heysel* - Vanderkindere

○ Station

Arrêt de surface, *bovengrondse halte*, aboveground stop

© 14-1789- STIB-MIVB - 03/2014

Roodebeek · Vandervelde · Alma · *Krainem* / Crainhem

1 Stockel / *Stokkel*

Diamant · Tomberg · Gribaumont · Joséphine-Charlotte · Montgomery

Madou

Arts-Loi / *Kunst-Wet* · Maalbeek / Maelbeek · Schuman · Merode

Georges Henri

Boileau

Thieffry

Trône / *Troon*

Naamsepoort / Porte de Namur

Pétillon

Louise / *Louiza*

Hankar

Munthof / Hôtel des Monnaies

Delta · Beaulieu · Demey

Sint-Gillisvoorplein / Parvis de Saint-Gilles

5 Herrmann-Debroux

Horta

Albert

7 Vanderkindere

3 Churchill

MIVB STIB

.brussels

Berlitz®

speaking your language

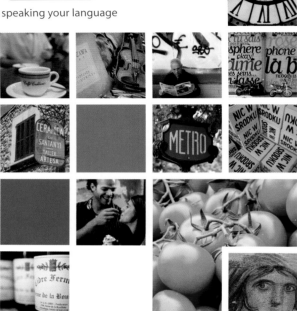

phrase book & dictionary
phrase book & CD

Available in: Arabic, Brazilian Portuguese*, Burmese*, Cantonese
Chinese, Croatian, Czech*, Danish*, Dutch, English, Filipino, Finnish*, French,
German, Greek, Hebrew*, Hindi*, Hungarian*, Indonesian, Italian, Japanese,
Korean, Latin American Spanish, Malay, Mandarin Chinese, Mexican Spanish,
Norwegian, Polish, Portuguese, Romanian*, Russian, Spanish, Swedish, Thai,
Turkish, Vietnamese
*Book only